DEPOSITIONS IN A NUTSHELL®

THIRD EDITION

PAUL B. BERGMAN
Professor of Law Emeritus
University of California, Los Angeles

JASON A. LIGHT
Lecturer in Law
University of California, Los Angeles

DAVID BABBE
Lecturer in Law
University of California, Los Angeles

WEST ACADEMIC

860 Blue Gentian Road, Suite 350
Eagan, MN 55121
1-877-888-1330

Published in the United States of America

ISBN: 978-1-68561-504-8

FOREWORD TO THE THIRD EDITION

This Nutshell focuses primarily on questioning strategies for deposing adverse deponents. In addition the book explains strategies for deposing friendly and neutral deponents, as well as how to effectively prepare clients and witnesses to have their depositions taken by adversaries.

Our aim is to provide practical suggestions and illustrations that will help you accomplish four primary deposition goals:

- Obtain and lock deponents into their stories;
- Search for and confirm helpful evidence;
- Uncover and undermine harmful testimony; and
- Advance your settlement position.

This third edition is based on the latest version of the rules set forth in the Federal Rules of Civil Procedure. We do however include references to common circumstances in which state rules may vary.

This third edition is more than an update to current rules. We have re-written and re-organized the entire text in ways that we hope make the book more concise and reader-friendly. This new edition also recognizes that many depositions are taken "remotely," that many records are stored electronically, and that many depositions are visually-recorded.

Many attorneys have taken advantage of the absence of "neutrals" from depositions to try to bully deponents as well as opposing counsel. This new edition therefore includes suggestions that we hope brings more "civility" to the deposition process.

Whether you are a law student, a novice lawyer or a lawyer who has taken many depositions, we hope that you find this new edition of the Nutshell helpful and at least occasionally enjoyable to read.

OUTLINE

FOREWORD TO THE THIRD EDITION III

Chapter 1. Overview **1**
1. Primary Deposition Goals 1
2. Questioning Strategies 2
3. Civility 3

Chapter 2. Arranging for Depositions **9**
1. Whom May You Depose? 9
2. Number of Depositions 9
3. Length of Depositions 9
4. Necessity of a Notice 10
5. Contents of a Notice 11
6. Where You May Take Depositions 11
7. When You May Take Depositions 12
8. Securing a Deponent's Attendance 13
9. Who May Attend 14
10. Arranging for Document Production 14
    A. Production at a Deposition 14
    B. Production Prior to a Deposition 14
11. Ensuring a Presiding Officer's Attendance 15
12. Ensuring That a Deposition Is Recorded 16
13. Waiving FRCP Requirements 16

Chapter 3. Deposition Preparation **17**
1. Identify Crucial Factual Contentions 17

2. Identify Important Topics, Events and Materials ... 20
   A. Technique # 1—Review Documents, Deposition Transcripts, and Discovery Responses ... 20
   B. Technique # 2—Review a Case Chronology ... 22
   C. Technique # 3—Use an Expert ... 25
   D. Technique # 4—Anticipate Your Cross Examination ... 26
   E. Technique # 5—Use a Pre-Fab Checklist ... 27
   F. Technique # 6—Internet Searches to Gather Background Information About the Deponent ... 29
3. Prepare a Deposition Outline ... 29
   A. How Should You Organize Your Outline? ... 29
   B. Should You Use Questioning Prompts or Specific Questions in Your Outline? ... 31
   C. How Detailed Should Your Outline Be? ... 35
   D. Strategic Decisions to Make During the Deposition Preparation Process ... 35
      1. Should You Omit Topics to Avoid Educating Your Opposition? ... 35
      2. Should You Avoid Putting Harmful Evidence on the Record? ... 36
      3. Can You Enhance Your Client's Settlement Position? ... 37
   E. Do You Need to Prioritize to Comply with the Seven-Hour Rule? ... 38

Chapter 4. Beginning and Concluding Depositions 39
1. Beginning Depositions 39
   A. Stipulations 39
   B. Admonitions 41
   C. Questions Regarding a Deponent's Preparation 53
      1. Documents a Deponent Used to Refresh Recollection 53
      2. Persons with Whom a Deponent Talked 56
   D. Background Questioning 56
      1. Employment History 57
      2. Educational Background 58
   E. Prior Experience Testifying at a Deposition or Trial 59
2. Concluding Depositions 59

Chapter 5. Timeline Questioning 63
1. Timeline Questioning Basics 64
2. An Illustrative Example 70
3. Overcoming Common Timeline Challenges 72
   A. Problem: A Deponent Cannot Organize Important Events Chronologically 72
   B. Problem: Overly-Broad Topics 72
   C. Problem: Overly-Broad Responses 73
   D. Problem: Side-Tracking 74

Chapter 6. T-Funnel Questioning 77
1. The T-Funnel Questioning Pattern 78
   A. An Illustration of the T-Funnel Pattern 79
   B. Using a Series of T-Funnels 82
2. "Parking" Subjects for Later Inquiry 86

3. Inverted T-Funnels 86
4. Common T-Funnels 88
   A. "Everything That Happened" T-Funnels 88
   B. "Everything You Did or Said" T-Funnels 90
   C. "All the Reasons" T-Funnels 91
   D. "Basis for a Conclusion, Opinion or Belief" T-Funnels 91
   E. "Helpful Information" T-Funnels 92
5. Event by Event Questioning: Combining Timelines with T-Funnels 93
6. Eliciting Stories When a Deponent Cannot Remember the Order of Events 100

Chapter 7. Strategies for Pinning the Tale on the Deponent 107
1. Fill in the Blanks 107
   A. Historical Reconstruction 108
   B. "Especially and Except When" 109
2. Pursue Hearsay and Speculation 110
3. Ask "Why" and "Why Not" 111
4. Ask "Have You Now Told Me Everything?" 112
5. Seek out Opinions and Their Bases 112
6. Press for Details 113
7. Parse Clumped Events 114
8. Seek Examples of Repeated Behavior 115
9. Clarify Ambiguous References and Gestures 116

Chapter 8. Cementing Helpful Answers 119
1. Pin down Helpful Answers 119
2. Cement "Surrounding Evidence" 122
3. Delay Cementing 122
4. Use the Deponent's Own Words 122

5. Offer a Neutral Explanation for Cementing 122
6. Accredit Helpful Information 123
7. Obtain an Evidentiary Foundation 124
8. Cement "That's All" 124
9. "Asked and Answered" Objections 125
10. Communicate Arguments 125

Chapter 9. Undermining Harmful Testimony 129
1. Should You Probe Credibility? 129
2. Strategies for Challenging Deponents' Credibility 131
   A. Challenge the Accuracy 131
   B. Attack the Inference 140
   C. Aggrandize the Lie 142
   D. Undermine Opinions, Conclusions, and Behavior over Time 143

Chapter 10. Responding to Evasive, Forgetful or Uncertain Deponents 147
1. Evasive Deponents 147
   A. Non-Responsive Answers 147
   B. Summary Conclusions 149
   C. "What Do You Mean by. . ." Answers 150
   D. Overly Literal or Hyper-Technical Deponents 152
      1. Avoid Making Your Questions Too Narrow 152
      2. Use a Series of Questions Containing Synonyms 153
      3. Ask for Information from All Sources 154

2. Responding to "I Can't Remember," "I'm Not Sure" and "I Don't Know" 155

Chapter 11. Managing Exhibits 161
1. Maintain a Clear Record 161
2. Authenticate an Exhibit 166
3. Diagrams 167

Chapter 12. Making and Responding to Objections and Instructions Not to Answer 171
1. Making Objections 171
   A. Purpose of Objections 171
   B. "Curable" and "Non- Curable" Objections 172
      1. Objections That Commonly Are Curable 172
      2. Common "Incurable" Objections That You Can Raise Later Even if You Don't Make Them at Deposition 178
   C. Forgoing Objections 179
   D. Phrasing Objections Properly 180
2. Responding to Objections 181
3. Instructions Not to Answer 183
4. Responding to Invalid Instructions Not to Answer 184
   A. On the Record, Ask Your Adversary to Withdraw the Instruction 184
   B. Put the Deponent's Refusal to Answer on the Record 185
   C. Determine the Scope of the Instruction Not to Answer 185

D. Obtain an Order Compelling an Answer ... 191
5. Responding to Inappropriate Behavior by Opposing Counsel ... 193
6. A Cautionary Note About Protective Orders ... 196

Chapter 13. FRCP 30(b)(6) "Subject Matter" Depositions ... 199
1. Why Take a Subject Matter Deposition? ... 199
2. How Many 30(b)(6) Depositions Can You Take? ... 200
3. The Importance of Comprehensive 30(b)(6) Notices ... 200
4. Questioning 30(b)(6) Designees ... 201
A. Is the Designee Knowledgeable? ... 201
B. Inquire About an Entity's Actions Rather than a Designee's ... 206
5. Going Beyond the Subjects in a Notice ... 207
6. Can You Depose a 30(b)(6) Designee Twice? ... 207
7. Using a 30(b)(6) Deposition to Obtain the Bases for an Adverse Party's Legal Contentions ... 209

Chapter 14. "Practices and Policies" Questioning Strategies ... 211
1. Distinguishing "Practices" from "Policies" ... 212
2. Purposes of Practice and Policy Inquiries ... 213
3. Whom to Depose ... 214
4. Questioning Strategies Regarding Practices ... 216
A. Responding to "It Depends" Answers ... 216

B. Inquire About Exceptions ... 218
C. Inquire About Prior and Subsequent Changes ... 221
D. Distinguish Between the Entity's Practice and That of the Deponent ... 222
5. Questioning Strategies Regarding Policies ... 223
6. Inquiring About Discrepancies Between Practices and Policies ... 226
7. Inquiring About Discrepancies Between Practices & Policies and What Happened in Your Client's Case ... 226

Chapter 15. Deposing Experts ... 227
1. Mandatory Disclosures ... 228
2. Beginning Adverse Expert Depositions ... 229
A. Give Admonitions ... 229
B. Confirm That You Have All Relevant Materials ... 230
C. Elicit Background Information ... 231
3. Elicit a Chronology of Case-Related Activities ... 233
4. Elicit All Opinions ... 237
5. Elicit the Basis for Each Opinion ... 239
A. Elicit the Evidentiary Basis for Each Opinion ... 240
B. Elicit the Specialized Knowledge Underlying Each Opinion ... 240
6. Undermining an Expert Opinion ... 242
7. Challenge #1—an Expert's Specialized Knowledge Is Inadequate ... 242
8. Challenge #2—"Exceptions" Detract from an Opinion's Accuracy ... 246

9. Challenge #3—Conflicting Authorities Undermine an Opinion 250
10. Challenge #4—an Opinion Is Based on Inaccurate Information from Third Parties ("Garbage in, Garbage out") 252
11. Challenge #5—Undermine the Results of Scientific Tests or Technical Procedures 256
12. Challenge #6—an Investigation Is Incomplete or Untimely 258
13. Challenge #7—an Expert Is Biased 259
14. Garner Support for Your Expert's Opinion 261
15. Opposing Party's Duty to Supplement Expert's Deposition Testimony 262
16. Preparing Your Own Expert for Deposition 263
17. Deposing Percipient Experts 263

Chapter 16. Preparing Deponents 269

1. Pre-Meeting Preparation 269
   A. Review the Validity of Document Requests 269
   B. Review Pertinent Documents 269
   C. Prepare a Case Chronology 270
   D. Help Identify the Person(s) Most Knowledgeable for Depositions of Entities 270
   E. Arrange to Meet the Client 271
2. Tell Clients What Documents to Review (and Not Review) 271
3. Conducting Preparation Meetings 272
   A. Explain What the Meeting Entails 273
   B. Review a Client's Version of Events 273

C. Briefly Explain What Will Occur During the Deposition 274
D. Explain the "Golden Rules" for Answering Questions 275
E. Discuss Objections and Instructions Not to Answer 279
F. Conduct a Practice Session 279
1. Devote Practice Questioning to Selected Topics 280
2. Ask Questions as Deposing Counsel 280
3. Improve Answers with Feedback and Advice 281
G. Concluding Preparation Sessions 284
4. Preparation Meetings with Non-Clients 285

Chapter 17. Deposing Friendly or Neutral Witnesses 289
1. Preparation Strategies 289
2. Background Questioning 290
3. Conform Testimony to Evidence Rules 290
4. Rhetorical Stories 291
5. Omitting Portions of Stories 293
6. Redirect Examination 293

INDEX 295

DEPOSITIONS
IN A NUTSHELL®

THIRD EDITION

CHAPTER 1

OVERVIEW

This Nutshell focuses on questioning strategies for effectively deposing adverse witnesses, as well as on the procedural rules that govern the deposition process. This chapter provides an introduction to the goals commonly pursued at deposition, as well as a preview of essential questioning skills and a discussion of the role of civility in depositions.

1. PRIMARY DEPOSITION GOALS

You typically pursue four primary goals when deposing adverse witnesses:

- Obtain a deponent's story;
- Search for and confirm helpful evidence;
- Uncover and undermine harmful testimony; and
- Advance your settlement position.

Perhaps the most common of these primary goals is to obtain and lock deponents into trial stories.[1] Eliciting a deponent's version of events enables you to assess the strength of that deponent's testimony should the case progress to trial. This will help you anticipate what direct examination of the witness might look like at trial, as well as give you a useful

---

1 Depositions cannot prevent witnesses from changing their stories at trial. But deposition testimony constitutes prior inconsistent statements that you can use to impeach the credibility of witness who change their stories.

basis upon which to prepare for cross examination. Moreover, learning a deponent's story also enables you to identify critical factual disputes, which can help direct your subsequent discovery efforts.

As you elicit a deponent's version of events, you also affirmatively attempt to identify and confirm helpful evidence that supports your client's legal claims. Deponents may reveal helpful evidence as they testify to their version of events. But often you need to separately inquire about specific topics that might provide helpful evidence.

As their stories unfold, adverse deponents usually testify to evidence that harms your legal claims. However, to avoid being blind-sided by unexpected facts during settlement negotiations or at trial you may also want to find out whether a deponent can provide additional harmful evidence. You then have a chance to undermine the damaging facts and adjust your settlement posture if harmful information is too damaging to overcome entirely.

Finally, deposition questioning may affect an adversary's settlement posture. For example, leading questions based on information that supports your client's legal claims might demonstrate both to a deponent and opposing counsel the strength of your case should the case proceed to trial.

2. QUESTIONING STRATEGIES

Effective deposition questioning rests on using a variety of questioning strategies. Chapter 5 focuses on Timeline questioning, which helps you to uncover a deponent's version of events in chronological order. Similarly, once you identify a topic or event, a combination of open and closed and/or leading questions can help you obtain a deponent's complete testimony on that topic or event. Chapter 6's discussion of T-funnels provides a questioning strategy for thorough probing of deponents' stories. Ensuing chapters focus on additional questioning techniques for pursuing the four primary deposition goals described above.

Together, the questioning strategies help you to establish a detailed record that locks deponents into their stories. For example, assume that during a deposition, you ask a deponent, "What did you have for breakfast that morning?" The deponent answers, "Grits." Then at trial the deponent testifies, "I saw the defendant enter a bar when I started to cook my grits and leave the store with bottles of vodka five minutes later when I sat down to eat my grits." You seek to impeach the "five minute" claim by asking, "Isn't it true that it takes 20 minutes for grits to cook until they are soft enough to eat?" The witness destroys your attempt at impeachment by answering, "I had instant grits that morning. They cook in five minutes."[2] The deposition record was not sufficiently detailed to lock the witness into the story!

3. CIVILITY

Opposing counsel may use hostile and unprofessional behavior in an attempt to thwart your

[2] The example is drawn from the courtroom comedy classic, *My Cousin Vinny* (1992).

attempts to pursue your deposition goals. Canon 7 of the American Bar Association Model Code provides, "A lawyer should represent a client zealously within the bounds of the law." Though Canon 7 embodies a core value of the adversary system, many legal commentators argue that an over-zealous reliance on Canon 7 accounts for the incivility (or bullying) that is increasingly part of the deposition process. Even though many depositions are visually-recorded, factors such as the absence of a judge, judges' frequent reluctance to sanction lawyers for intemperate deposition behavior, and lawyers' desire to demonstrate to clients that they are "fighting" for them all-too-often combine to produce a toxic atmosphere at depositions. Sadly, the result is that lawyers sometimes behave in a way that first grade teachers wouldn't tolerate in their students. For example:

- A lawyer may make inappropriate objections and issue improper instructions not to answer.
- A lawyer may ignore scheduling needs and refuse a reasonable request to re-schedule a deposition, forcing an adversary to seek relief from a judge.
- Lawyers may resort to rude language. For example, in *In re First City Bancorp of Texas* (282 F.3d 864 (5th Cir. 2002)), during a deposition a lawyer referred on the record to opposing counsel as a stooge, a puppet, a deadhead and an underling who graduated from a bottom-feeding law school.

- Lawyers may use delaying tactics so as to maximize the inconvenience and cost of litigation. For example, the case of *GMAC v. HTFC Corp.* (252 F.R.D. 253 (E.D. PA 2008)) quotes a deponent's deposition response in which the deponent (on the advice of the deponent's lawyer) provided a lengthy and meandering answer and then in response to the deposing attorney's protest stated on the record, "I'm going to keep going. I'll have you flying in and out of New York City every single month and this will go on for years. And by the way, along the way GMAC will be bankrupt and I will laugh at you."

In response to the frequency of embarrassing and unprofessional behavior, legislators and bar associations in many jurisdictions have developed civility guidelines. For example:

The "Principles of Civility, Integrity and Professionalism" adopted by ABOTA (the American Board of Trial Advocacy, a national group of experienced trial lawyers committed to civility and justice) are "intended to discourage conduct that demeans, hampers or obstructs our system of justice." Principle 19 states that attorneys should "never take depositions for the purpose of harassment or to burden an opponent with increased litigation expenses."

The Preamble of Utah's "Standards of Professionalism and Civility" states, "A lawyer's conduct should be characterized at all times by personal courtesy and professional integrity.

Moreover, conduct that may be characterized as uncivil, abrasive, abusive, hostile or obstructive impedes the fundamental goal of resolving disputes rationally, peacefully and efficiently."

California's "Attorney Guidelines of Civility and Professionalism" include provisions pertaining to the taking of depositions that forbid the use of foul and hostile language, the practice of scheduling depositions without prior contact for convenient times and locations, and rude-toned and intimidating questioning. And federal courts have enforced civility rules at deposition.

The scope and enforceability of a "civility code" can vary widely from one jurisdiction to another. However, among the professional practices you can follow during the deposition process to practice civility include:

- Using a calm, measured, respectful tone of voice throughout a deposition, whether addressing a deponent or opposing counsel.
- Allowing deponents to complete answers before propounding additional questions.
- Refraining from personal invective and snide remarks.

Your ability to obtain a protective order and/or sanctions against opposing counsel who behave inappropriately may well depend on the propriety of your own deposition behavior. Adhering to civility rules or guidelines can improve your chances of success should a judge have occasion to examine a visual recording or a written deposition transcript in connection with your motion for a protective order and sanctions. And of course, civility is itself a value; civility among lawyers tends to enhance respect for the legal system and the legal profession.

Civility is fully consistent with your ethical obligations to be an advocate for your client. You can use all the questioning strategies described in this book, including pressing deponents to provide complete details, encouraging deponents to provide helpful evidence, undermining the credibility of harmful evidence, and communicating arguments to a deponent, while remaining civil. You can and should be persistent and thorough; but antagonism or nastiness is unnecessary, often counterproductive, and inconsistent with the aspirational and increasingly enforceable norms of the legal profession.

And civility may promote your rhetorical goals! Perhaps adverse counsel has warned a deponent, "The deposing lawyer is your enemy, not your friend. The lawyer will try to bully you and trick you and attack your testimony by twisting everything you say by putting words in your mouth. Answer as briefly as you can, one-word answers as much as possible, and never volunteer anything." You may counter these dire warnings by practicing civility. If you put deponents at ease by demonstrating that you are a calm, decent person who cares about the truth and the deponents' well-being, deponents may be more likely to provide more complete narrative answers that include information that advances your legal claims.

CHAPTER 2

ARRANGING FOR DEPOSITIONS

This chapter briefly reviews common procedures for arranging for depositions under the Federal Rules of Civil Procedure.

1. WHOM MAY YOU DEPOSE?

You can depose anyone who may have information relevant to the claims or defenses in a lawsuit. The roster of potential deponents includes:

- Parties to a case;
- Non-party individuals;
- Non-party entities such as partnerships, public or private corporations and government agencies; and
- Experts who an adversary may call to testify at trial.

2. NUMBER OF DEPOSITIONS

Absent a court order or a written stipulation among the parties, a party may take no more than ten depositions. Moreover, absent court approval or a written stipulation from all adverse parties, you may not depose a person more than once in the same case.

3. LENGTH OF DEPOSITIONS

Absent a court order or a stipulation, a deposition is limited to a single day of no more than seven (7) hours of testimony. Breaks and recesses do not count towards the seven hours.

4. NECESSITY OF A NOTICE

Before you depose a party or non-party, you must serve every other party with reasonable written notice of your intention to take the deposition. If your advance notice to a deponent is unreasonably short, the deponent can properly refuse to attend a deposition. Moreover, if you fail to provide notice to a party, or if the length of advance notice to a party is unreasonably short, you will be unable to use any deposition testimony against a party who was not present or represented at the deposition. In addition, if you fail to properly notice a deposition, and as a result the deponent fails to attend but other noticed parties do attend, a judge can order you to pay the reasonable expenses incurred by the attending parties, including attorney's fees.

It is both good practice and professionally courteous to clear the times and places for depositions with opposing counsel whenever possible. Doing so before you send out a deposition notice typically saves time and aggravation. After all, if you do not cooperate with other parties in this way, they may well respond in like manner by scheduling their own depositions at times and places that are inconvenient for you or your client or by seeking protective orders pursuant to FRCP 26(c).

5. CONTENTS OF A NOTICE

At a minimum, a Notice of Deposition must set forth the following information:

- The date, time and place of a deposition.
- The name and address of each person to be deposed. If you are deposing an entity pursuant to FRCP 30(b)(6) and you do not know the name of the person to be deposed, you need only a general description sufficient to identify the examinee or the particular class or group to which the examinee belongs. For example, you might refer to a 30(b)(6) deponent as "the person most knowledgeable with respect to the Health Department's June 12 inspection of the premises at 1053 Hanley Avenue."
- The method of recording the testimony. Testimony is most commonly recorded stenographically. However, either in lieu of or addition to a stenographic record, you may specify that a deposition will be visually recorded or sound recorded.
- If pursuant to FRCP 30(b)(6) you intend to depose an entity such as a partnership or corporation, the notice must identify the subjects that you will explore at deposition.

6. WHERE YOU MAY TAKE DEPOSITIONS

Typically you can depose a party in the district where an action has been brought. However, you must normally notice a non-party's deposition for a location which is no more than 100 miles away from the place where the non-party deponent resides, is employed or regularly transacts business in person. FRCP 45(a) mandates that a Subpoena recite this limitation. Agents of non-party corporations ordinarily must be deposed within the district where the corporation has its principal place of business.

Deposing counsel typically have held depositions in their own offices. However, you may notice a deposition for a site other than your office for such reasons as:

- Your office is not located in a proper district. For example, if you must depose a non-party deponent in a different district, the deposition may take place in the suite of a hotel located in the proper district.
- You want to visually record a deposition, and your office lacks proper video facilities. In this instance, you may notice the deposition for the office of the videographer who oversees the videotaping.

You may also elect to take a deposition remotely by telephone or video conference rather than in person.

7. WHEN YOU MAY TAKE DEPOSITIONS

Absent a court order or a written stipulation, you generally cannot take a deposition until after you and your adversary have met and developed a joint discovery plan pursuant to FRCP 26(f) and the court has issued a Scheduling Order pursuant to FRCP

16(b). Typically, such an order issues within 90 days after the first defendant's appearance and within 120 days after a defendant has been served with a complaint.

The FRCP do not provide for priorities in the taking of depositions. Unless you are precluded from doing so by a Scheduling Order, and except with respect to expert witnesses, you can proceed to take depositions at whatever time and in whatever order you choose. That another party may have already noticed a deposition does not deprive you of the right to notice an earlier deposition of a different deponent.

8. SECURING A DEPONENT'S ATTENDANCE

When a deponent is a party (or an officer, director or managing agent of a party), the only pre-deposition task you must complete in order to compel the party's attendance is to serve a proper Notice of Deposition. For parties, notices sent by traditional mail or electronically-mailed notice generally suffices.

You can compel a non-party deponent to attend a deposition only through personal service of either a Subpoena re Deposition and/or a Subpoena Duces Tecum re Deposition. Use the latter if a non-party deponent is to bring documents to a deposition. To compel a non-party deponent to appear, you must also tender witness fees.

9. WHO MAY ATTEND

In addition to the deponent, attorneys for each party, court reporter and videographer (if the deposition is video recorded), the parties, and when a corporation is a defendant, corporate officers, are generally entitled to attend a deposition. If you wish to prevent others from attending a deposition, you may move for a protective order.

10. ARRANGING FOR DOCUMENT PRODUCTION

A. PRODUCTION AT A DEPOSITION

If you want a party deponent to bring documents to a deposition, identify those documents in the Notice of Deposition. However, you must then serve the Notice of Deposition on the party at least thirty days in advance of the deposition.

To obtain documents from a non-party deponent, serve the deponent with a Subpoena Duces Tecum re Deposition. The documents to be produced at the deposition should be described in the Subpoena Duces Tecum re Deposition or in a separate attachment which must be served along with the Subpoena. To compel a non-party deponent to appear, you must also tender witness fees.

B. PRODUCTION PRIOR TO A DEPOSITION

Questioning at deposition with respect to documents is likely to be more effective if you have reviewed the documents in advance of the deposition.

Often, a party's mandatory disclosures include documents that you can examine in advance of a deposition. In addition, you may secure further documents in advance of a deposition from a party by making a Request for Production under FRCP 34.

To obtain documents prior to a deposition from a non-party, serve the non-party with a Subpoena Duces Tecum that requires the non-party to produce specified documents for inspection and copying at the time and place designated in the Subpoena. You must give prior written notice to all other parties regarding the time and place that the documents are to be produced. After reviewing the documents, you can then decide whether you want to depose the non-party. Initially subpoenaing only the documents is particularly useful when a non-party is an entity whose only connection to a case seems to be that it possesses relevant documents.

11. ENSURING A PRESIDING OFFICER'S ATTENDANCE

When you notice a deposition you are responsible for ensuring the attendance of a presiding officer, who is a person authorized to swear in the deponent. A person who can administer the oath is an officer authorized to administer oaths by the laws of the United States or of the place where the examination is held, or before a person appointed by the court in which the action is pending. Typically a presiding officer is also a certified court reporter who can both administer the oath and stenographically record the deposition.

To carry out your responsibility be sure to make prior arrangements with a court officer to be present at the time and place set for the deposition. Should you fail to do so and no one is present to administer the oath, you may be sanctioned if other parties appear at the deposition ready to proceed.

12. ENSURING THAT A DEPOSITION IS RECORDED

If you notice a deposition, you are responsible to make sure that it is recorded. As noted above, a deposition may be recorded stenographically or in a variety of other ways. If your chosen method is other than stenographic recordation, the method must be one from which a stenographic record can subsequently be made.

13. WAIVING FRCP REQUIREMENTS

Parties have broad latitude to enter into stipulations modifying the FRCP provisions relating to deposition arrangements and other discovery methods. For example, you might stipulate with opposing counsel that a deposition may be taken on 2 days' notice. Stipulations modifying the provisions of the FRCP should generally either be stated on the deposition record or memorialized in a separate writing.

CHAPTER 3

DEPOSITION PREPARATION

This chapter describes preparation strategies and techniques to help you accomplish the four primary deposition goals: obtain a deponent's version of significant events; search for and confirm helpful evidence; uncover and seek to undermine harmful evidence; and improve your client's settlement position.

The preparation process consists of three main activities:

- Identify crucial factual contentions;
- Identify the topics, events and materials to explore: and
- Prepare a deposition outline.

Not all depositions will justify your pursuing the full panoply of preparation techniques that this chapter describes. You can pick and choose. preparation strategies depending on such factors as the preparation you've already done in connection with earlier depositions or discovery, your litigation budget, a case's value and complexity, your litigation experience, and a deposition's importance.

1. IDENTIFY CRUCIAL FACTUAL CONTENTIONS

Factual contentions are the parties' specific factual conclusions that you seek to support or undermine. For both plaintiffs and defendants, most cases consist of a limited number of crucial factual contentions. Factual contentions are crucial when they are disputed and substantively pivotal. Such contentions largely determine the evidence that you pursue during depositions and all other discovery. Therefore if you haven't already done so begin to prepare for a deposition by identifying crucial factual contentions. These contentions will typically fall into one of the following three categories.

- **Elements from Causes of Action or Affirmative Defenses**

Substantive rules are of course the backbone of many factual contentions.

Example: In a fraudulent misrepresentation case, one legal element that a plaintiff must prove is that a defendant "knowingly" made a false statement. One crucial factual contention with respect to this element for a plaintiff might be, "When the defendant told my client that XYZ Corp. had a signed contract for the distribution of a new software system, the defendant knew that the contract had not been signed." In the same case, one crucial factual contention for the defense might be, "When the defendant told Plaintiff that XYZ Corp. had a signed contract for the distribution of a new software system, the defendant believed that statement to be true."

Example: In an age discrimination case, one of plaintiff's crucial factual contentions might be, "The plaintiff was discharged because the employer wanted to save money by hiring a younger, less experienced replacement at a lower salary." In the same case, one of the defendant's crucial contentions might be, "The defendant discharged the plaintiff because she was repeatedly insubordinate to her supervisor."

- **Pivotal Evidentiary Disputes**

Crucial factual contentions may focus on evidentiary disputes.

Example: In a sexual harassment case, the plaintiff claims that two months prior to her discharge she declined her supervisor's request for a date; the supervisor denies ever asking the plaintiff for a date. The crucial factual contention for plaintiff might be, "The supervisor asked plaintiff for a date prior to discharging her." The defendant's crucial factual contention in that same case may be, "The supervisor never asked plaintiff for a date."

Example: In a breach of contract case, the defendant claims he never signed an agreement. Plaintiff argues she has a copy of an agreement that defendant did in fact sign. A crucial factual contention for the defendant is, "The defendant's signature on the agreement was a forgery." On the other hand, one of plaintiff's crucial factual contentions is, "The defendant's signature on the agreement was genuine."

• **"Extra-Legal" Contentions**

Emotional factors often contribute to the outcomes of legal disputes. When appropriate, you may develop factual contentions that capture the empathic aspects of disputes.

> Example: In a case against police officers for using unreasonable force when effectuating an arrest, the plaintiff may seek to prove that the police stopped the plaintiff only because he was a "racial outsider" driving alone in what the police considered a "high crime area."

2. IDENTIFY IMPORTANT TOPICS, EVENTS AND MATERIALS

Once you have identified crucial factual contentions, you can use one or more of the following techniques to identify areas of inquiry that might lead to helpful or harmful evidence relating to each contention. Remember, you need not pursue each and every preparation technique described below in every single deposition; instead, this list of techniques provides you with a menu of alternatives.

A. TECHNIQUE # 1—REVIEW DOCUMENTS, DEPOSITION TRANSCRIPTS, AND DISCOVERY RESPONSES

As a general matter, most lawyers wait to begin taking depositions until an adversary has made voluntary disclosures and responded to requests for production of documents. (The "one deposition per person" rule makes it risky to take important depositions before you have obtained important documents). As a result, when you prepare to take a deposition, you are likely to have a significant number of documents from a variety of sources—from your client, from the opposing party, from third parties that have responded to subpoenas, and potentially witness statements and reports from investigators or experts. In addition you may have transcripts from prior depositions taken in the case and responses from the opposing party to your interrogatories and requests for admissions. You should review these documents, deposition transcripts, and discovery responses as you prepare for a deposition to identify:

- Helpful evidence that you want the deponent to confirm.
- Harmful evidence that you hope to undermine.
- Questions you have concerning such matters as how and why a document was prepared, to whom it was distributed and the significance of topics and events to which a document refers.

If a case file contains thousands or even hundreds of documents, you may not have time to read each and every document before taking a deposition. Moreover, many documents may be unrelated to the deposition you are about to take. Therefore, to prepare for a given deposition, you will usually have to cull through documents to determine which ones you want to examine in detail.

If you have a computerized litigation support system that contains a database composed of an abstract for each document or deposition transcript in your file, the culling process may not prove difficult. You can quickly develop a list of keywords that you, an associate and/or a paralegal can use to search the document database. One keyword will of course be the name of the person to be deposed. As a general matter, you should do a preliminary review of all documents that were authored by, sent to, or reference the person you will depose. Other keywords will be those that you believe relate to your crucial contentions. Finally, consider whether you can further cull documents by excluding those outside a certain time period.

After you have winnowed the number of documents to a manageable number, review those documents to identify events and topics that you want to cover during the deposition. You should also review the deposition excerpts relating to those events and topics to see what other deponents have said about them. And you should review the other side's discovery responses to see if the deponent has verified those responses or if the deponent is identified as someone having personal knowledge about the substance of the responses.

B. TECHNIQUE # 2—REVIEW A CASE CHRONOLOGY

Case chronologies can be a powerful tool for organizing and using information that you obtain in the discovery process. While formats for a case chronology tend to vary from one lawyer to another, a useful case chronology typically incorporates four types of information:

- All parties' versions of important events, listed as much as possible in chronological order.
- The approximate or precise dates when important events occurred.
- The documents, individuals and/or other sources that provide support for the important events.
- An indication of disputes in the parties' version of events.

The following illustrative example of a small portion of a case chronology involves a lawsuit by the National Resources Defense Council ("NRDC") against a county for failing to take adequate measures to keep toxic materials at a county construction site out of storm water.

Date	**Event**	**Source**	**Disputes**
02/10/__	NRDC letter notifies County of Toxic Dirt Problem	NRDC letter 00004	
03/14/__	Depart. Road Maint. refers NRDC notice letter to Benson	County Memo 00104	

Date	Event	Source	Disputes
04/25/__	Smith of NRDC calls County Engineer, Helms, re: no response to Tox dirt letter	Smith memo 00023	Helms says Smith never called. Helms deposition Page 42 line 5
Late April	Benson tells Carson that NRDC is being unreasonable	Anders statement 04673	
05/14/__	Benson prepares memo on construct site visits. County inspectors are requiring the contractor to put down appropriate matting	Benson memo 01435	
06/10/__	Higgins tells Carson that Benson said sometimes county inspectors prepare reports without actually visiting the site	Carson memo 02234	

Review your case chronology and identify:

- Topics, events and documents to inquire into to flesh out the deponent's version of significant events. For example, as the NRDC's lawyer preparing to depose Benson, you would want to seek Benson's version of what happened during visits to the construction site. You also want to try to fill in any gaps in your chronology. For example, the chronology above might remind you as the NRDC's lawyer to probe the gap between 03/14/___ (when a letter was referred to Benson), and late April (when Benson spoke to Carson) when deposing Benson.

- Helpful evidence that you want the deponent to confirm.
- Harmful evidence that you hope to undermine.

C. TECHNIQUE # 3—USE AN EXPERT

Even when you are preparing for a lay witness deposition, your expert can often help you identify existing helpful or harmful evidence and topics that might produce additional evidence to support a crucial factual contention.

Consider this example. Your client has brought an unfair business practice case against a computer trade school that claims to train students to be computer programmers. One of your client's crucial contentions is that the classes did not cover the basic skills required to become a computer programmer. You are about to depose the school's educational director. When preparing for this deposition, you might well be able to identify helpful topics even without an expert's help. For example, you probably wouldn't need an expert's help to identify a topic such as the percentage of students who got jobs as computer programmers after graduation. However, an expert's help may produce such additional topics as:

- What computer languages are currently in wide use?
- What experience and training should teachers have so as to be able to teach these subjects effectively?
- What kinds of lab projects and drills should students be given in order to learn to program in these languages?
- What is the average salary of teachers who work in private, for-profit computer training schools?

An expert's answers to such questions will provide you with topics that you may inquire into at deposition.

While you may automatically think of an "expert" as a hired outsider, in some situations you may be able to look to your client or to a more experienced colleague as a source of expertise.

D. TECHNIQUE # 4—ANTICIPATE YOUR CROSS EXAMINATION

Another way to identify potentially useful areas of inquiry at deposition is to ask yourself, "What would I want to ask this deponent on cross-examination at trial?" Questions that you might ask yourself when using this approach include:

- "What evidence might I elicit on cross examination at trial to attack the deponent's credibility?"
- "Are there aspects of my adversary's version of events that seem implausible?" "If so, what evidence might I be able to elicit from this deponent to demonstrate that implausibility?"
- "What evidence would I like to bring out on cross from this deponent to support my affirmative case?"

E. TECHNIQUE # 5—USE A PRE-FAB CHECKLIST

Another approach for identifying areas of inquiry is to use a checklist drawn from a practice guide. A number of practitioner-oriented texts set out checklists that identify topics that pertain to specific types of cases. Here for example is a partial checklist that you might use in a lawsuit growing out of an automobile accident.

Pre-Accident Events

1. Activities earlier in the day
2. Food, alcohol, drugs
3. Physical condition at time

Events Immediately Preceding the Collision

1. Location and direction of the vehicles
2. Passenger
3. Traffic conditions

4. Visibility
5. Other distractions
6. Where first saw defendant's car
7. Marking diagram and photographs

Collision

1. Speed before impact
2. Traffic signals
3. Braking and other conduct of plaintiff
4. Braking and other conduct of defendant
5. Marking diagram and photographs

Post-Collision Events

1. Bystander activities
2. Police activities
3. What plaintiff and defendant did
4. What plaintiff and defendant said
5. Plaintiff's and defendant's condition after the accident
6. Ambulance

You may also be able to obtain a checklist from a friend or colleague who has extensive experience in a particular area of substantive law. For example, if you are taking your first deposition in a wrongful termination case or a construction defect case, you may want to ask colleagues with experience in these types of litigation for their deposition outlines or checklists.

F. TECHNIQUE # 6—INTERNET SEARCHES TO GATHER BACKGROUND INFORMATION ABOUT THE DEPONENT

You may benefit from learning about a deponent's background before a deposition. Such information may alert you to topics you might inquire into or help you assess the credibility of testimony that emerges at the deposition. You can use internet searches to obtain a host of pertinent information about a deponent, including prior experience, assets, civil and criminal court filings, judgments and liens, professional licenses, SEC filings, etc.

3. PREPARE A DEPOSITION OUTLINE

Once you have identified potential areas of inquiry, organize the information into a deposition outline. This section describes several issues you might want to consider as you prepare outlines.

A. HOW SHOULD YOU ORGANIZE YOUR OUTLINE?

While there are numerous ways to organize a deposition outline, one straightforward organizational scheme is to list areas of inquiry in three main categories: (1) Background; (2) Deponent's version of significant events; and (3) Strategically reserved areas of inquiry.

If you follow this organizational approach, inquiries relating to education, work experience, training, and other matters not directly relating to the case would be included in the "Background" section. Inquiries pursuing a deponent's version of significant events would be included in the "Version" section. You might want to list the areas of inquiry in the "Version" section chronologically, event by event. Areas of inquiry that you want to reserve for later in the deposition would be included in the "Strategically reserved" section. For example, you might choose to reserve questions that would be embarrassing or upsetting to the deponent, or questions designed to communicate arguments to the deponent and/or opposing counsel, until the end of the deposition in order to avoid disrupting rapport.

As a general matter, you will usually want to organize documents in chronological order in your outline. That is particularly true where documents describe or relate to events that you will be covering. For example, if you will be questioning a deponent about a particular board of director meeting, you will want to include any questions about written minutes of that meeting in the portion of your outline addressing the meeting.

Although you generally want to cover events and documents in your outline in chronological order, deciding when you should cover particular topics may be less clear. For example, in a traffic accident case, assume that you plan to ask the defendant about vision-related problems. One option would be to cover that topic as part of the "Background" section of the deposition; another option would be to cover that topic as part of the "Version" section when you question the defendant about what he saw as he approached the intersection. There is often no right or wrong answer about when to cover a particular topic, but if you are trying to avoid alerting a deponent about the potential significance of a particular topic, it may be helpful to cover the topic during the "Background" rather than the "Version" section of the deposition.

B. SHOULD YOU USE QUESTIONING PROMPTS OR SPECIFIC QUESTIONS IN YOUR OUTLINE?

Even for important areas of inquiry, trying to "script" your precise deposition questions rarely makes sense. Any script would have to correctly predict a deponent's answers. Moreover, scripted questions are likely to inhibit your ability to adjust to unexpected answers. Key skills for taking effective depositions are to listen to and watch a deponent carefully to a deponent's answers so you can quickly pursue unanticipated information. Reading questions from a deposition outline interferes with those strategies.

In lieu of writing out specific questions in outlines, consider including questioning prompts that provide you with a checklist of the information that you want to get about a particular event or topic. To illustrate how you might incorporate questioning prompts in an outline, consider the following example. Assume that you represent a plaintiff who was hit while in a crosswalk by a car driven by the defendant. You have learned from a police report that the defendant had been at a bar shortly before hitting your client. When you depose the defendant, you hope to obtain information supporting the factual contention that the defendant was impaired at the time of the accident.

It is often easier to think of the kinds of information that you want to get from the deponent in the quiet of your office than it is when you are under the gun at deposition. As you identify potential follow-up questions, include prompts in your outline that remind you of the information that you want to obtain. For example, your outline for topics in the pedestrian-in-the-crosswalk case might include such prompts as the following:

<u>Event: The Defendant at the bar.</u>

- Time arrived at bar
- Arrived with/met friends/colleagues
  - How many
  - Names/relationships
- Reason for going to bar
  - Celebration?
- Birthday
- Promotion
- Going away
- Sports

- Other
- All alcoholic drinks consumed while at bar (t-funnel)
    - Beer
- How many glasses/bottles/pitchers
- Type of beer
- Lager/IPA/other
- Alcohol content
    - Wine
- Type/amount
    - Hard alcohol
- Type/amount
    - Other alcohol
- Type/amount
- Drinking games?
- Who paid/how paid for drinks
- Happy hour?
    - Other discount drinks
- Consume any recreational/prescription drugs in bar (t-funnel)
    - Type/amount/dosage
- All food consumed (t-funnel)
- Time left bar

- Documentary evidence
    - Photos/videos
    - Social media postings
    - Credit card receipts
    - Anything else

. . . .

Many areas of inquiry commonly re-occur throughout a deposition. For example, as you pursue a deponent's version of events you may elicit testimony of similar events, e.g., a series of meetings or inspections. If so, you might develop a standard set of prompts that you can refer to each time a deponent mentions a similar event. Your standard prompts for a meeting might include:

When?

Where?

Who present?

In person/remote

Duration?

Purposes?

Topics discussed?

What happened?

Notes or records?

Agenda?

Meeting recorded?

Minutes?

Memo?

Emails?

You could include a prompt like "Ask Event Essentials" for each event you include in your outline rather than repeating these questions verbatim for every single meeting. Other re-occurring areas of inquiry for which you might develop standard sets of prompts include documents and conversations.

C. HOW DETAILED SHOULD YOUR OUTLINE BE?

How detailed an outline to prepare is ultimately a matter of what works best for you. You may be comfortable with relatively sparse outlines, relying on your ability to identify information "on the fly." But you instead may prefer the security of lengthier outlines that provide detailed sets of prompts. When you first start taking depositions, it is generally safer to err on the side of using a more detailed outline.

D. STRATEGIC DECISIONS TO MAKE DURING THE DEPOSITION PREPARATION PROCESS

1. Should You Omit Topics to Avoid Educating Your Opposition?

A common risk of deposing adverse witnesses is educating an opponent about your legal theories and factual contentions that have not yet been disclosed in discovery. For example:

- If you ask a deponent to explain an inconsistency between the deponent's testimony and the account of a friendly third-party witness, you reveal the conflict and perhaps encourage your adversary to seek evidence undermining the friendly witness' account.
- If your questions emphasize the importance of the time when an adverse party deponent became aware of information on which a lawsuit is based, you may prompt the deponent and opposing counsel to characterize events so as to eliminate your Statute of Limitations defense.
- Your adversary may be unaware of a document containing evidence that hurts your case. If you question a deponent with respect to such a document, you reveal the harmful information to your adversary.

In situations such as these, you have to make a strategic decision about whether the advantages of obtaining a fuller picture of and possibly undermining your adversary's case outweigh the risks of educating the opponent.

2. Should You Avoid Putting Harmful Evidence on the Record?

You ordinarily want to uncover harmful evidence at a deposition so that you can try to undermine it at the deposition or through further discovery. Nevertheless, if you think the deponent may be unavailable as a witness at trial, you may choose to omit questioning relating to harmful evidence. This strategy may prevent an adversary from reading harmful evidence from a transcript into the record when a deponent is unavailable at trial.

3. Can You Enhance Your Client's Settlement Position?

The vast majority of cases settle prior to trial. Consequently, if settlement is a reasonable possibility, you may want to consider what you can do at the deposition that might enhance the terms or likelihood of settlement. Obviously, to the extent that you obtain evidence to support your client's case or undermine the opposition's case, you tend to enhance the terms of settlement. Other factors you may want to consider to increase the possibility of a favorable settlement include:

- Ask questions that focus on your contentions' strengths;
- In multi-party cases, elicit testimony tending to shift the blame to another party. For example, if you represent one of multiple defendants, elicit testimony emphasizing the culpability or liability of a co-defendant. The deposition record may make the co-defendant recognize that its exposure at trial is greater than previously thought. As a result, the co-defendant may be more likely to make or sweeten a settlement offer.

- Seek information providing you with a window into an adverse party's underlying needs and concerns. To the extent that you can elicit information about such matters as an adverse party's economic circumstances and social values, you foster your ability to fashion settlement proposals that meet both parties' underlying needs. For example, if your questions reveal that an out-of-work opponent has been making earnest efforts to find employment, you may infer that the adversary has an immediate need for money and therefore might be especially anxious to settle.

E. DO YOU NEED TO PRIORITIZE TO COMPLY WITH THE SEVEN-HOUR RULE?

FRCP 30(d) provides that a deposition may not exceed one day of seven hours, absent a court order or a stipulation among the parties to extend the time. If you are subject to a time limitation for a deposition, you will want to adjust your outline to make sure that you cover the most important areas of inquiry during the allotted time.

CHAPTER 4

BEGINNING AND CONCLUDING DEPOSITIONS

This Chapter explores effective strategies for the beginning and ending phases of depositions.

1. BEGINNING DEPOSITIONS

Depositions typically begin with a court officer, usually a court reporter, putting on the record the officer's name and business address; the date, time and place of deposition; and the deponent's name. The officer then administers the oath to the deponent and identifies on the record all of the persons present.

After the court officer concludes these housekeeping details, the officer turns the deposition over to you.

A. STIPULATIONS

At the outset, one issue that you might want to address through stipulation concerns the time limits imposed by FRCP 30(d)(2). FRCP 30(d)(2) limits depositions to "one day of seven hours." Thus, you or any other party may terminate a deposition when it exceeds seven hours.

The FRCP 30(d)(2) time limit can be extended by a stipulation entered into by all parties or by a court order. Therefore, if you anticipate questioning a deponent for longer than "one day of seven hours" and haven't previously done so, you may at the outset of a deposition ask opposing counsel to stipulate to a waiver of the limitations of FRCP 30(d)(2). You can tailor stipulations to the circumstances of each case. For example, a stipulation may state that you have up to "one day of 10 hours" to complete a deposition, or that your deposition "is not subject to fixed time limits, but any party has the right to terminate the deposition and move the court for a protective order if the time of deposition is unduly prolonged in bad faith." Of course, be sure to read any such stipulation into the record.

If your adversary does not agree to waive the one day/seven hour time limit set forth in FRCP 30(d)(2), one alternative is to modify your questioning so as to fit within the limit. A second alternative is to use all of your allotted time, and then seek a court order extending the time limit if the opposing party continues to refuse to stipulate to an extension and you have not completed your questioning.

As a deposition proceeds, you or opposing counsel might propose a variety of stipulations. Such stipulations may relate to housekeeping matters such as the numbering of exhibits, or to more substantive matters such as the admissibility of documents. You are under no obligation to enter into stipulations at any point in a deposition, and of course should never do so if you are uncertain of what you are stipulating to. If you do agree to enter into a stipulation, better practice is to first go off the record, hash out the exact terms of the stipulation, and then read the terms into the record.

B. ADMONITIONS

After a deponent has been sworn and stipulations (if any) have been entered into the record, admonitions are the typical next phase of depositions. Admonitions are questions which review basic deposition procedures and inquire into a deponent's capacity to respond fully and accurately to your questions.

Admonitions serve a variety of purposes:

- Admonitions provide you with a basis for undermining common justifications that deponents tend to give for making changes in their deposition testimony or later giving testimony that conflicts with their deposition testimony.
- Admonitions help to put deponents at ease, thereby perhaps improving a deponent's ability to recall important events and details.
- Deponents may infer from your explanations of deposition procedures that you are fair and reasonable, and if so may respond more fully and cooperatively to your questions.

Set out below is a typical set of admonitions, followed by a discussion of their contents.

1. Q: Ms. Strauss, my name is Orin Parrent and I am the attorney for Mr. Flowers. I assume that your attorney has reviewed with you what will take place here today, but just so there won't be any misunderstanding, let me briefly describe what will happen. John Flowers has filed a

lawsuit concerning the loan secured by a deed of trust for the property at 9412 E. 88th Street. Today I will be asking you questions to learn information that might be relevant to that lawsuit. My questions and your answers will be taken down by the court reporter on this machine that you see in front of you. At the conclusion of the questioning, the court reporter will transcribe my questions and your answers into a booklet that will be known as your deposition transcript. Do you understand that?

2. A: Yes.

3. Q: The court reporter can't take down nods or shakes of the head so it's necessary for you to answer my questions audibly, all right?

4. A: I'll try.

5. Q: When I begin a question you may know what I'm going to ask before I finish my question, but it's easier for the court reporter to get everything down correctly if you let me finish my question before you start to answer. Will you try to do that?

6. A: Sure.

7. Q: Have you ever been deposed before, Ms. Strauss?

8. A: No, this is my first time.

9. Q: Do you understand that you were administered an oath by the court reporter and are testifying today under penalty of perjury?

10. A: Yes, I do.

11. Q: And do you understand that your deposition testimony has the same importance and significance it would have if you were testifying in court before a judge and a jury?

12. A: Yes.

13. Q: And you'll do your best to tell the complete truth at this deposition, won't you Ms. Strauss?

14. A: I will.

15. Q: If you don't understand a question you shouldn't answer it. Instead of answering a question you don't understand, please just tell me that you don't understand the question. Will you agree to do that?

16. A: Sure.

17. Q: So if you do answer a question, I will assume that you have understood the question and that you were giving me your best possible answer. Do you understand that?

18. A: Yes.

19. Q: Sometimes you will understand my question perfectly well, but you're not sure you know the answer because your answer is a guess or an estimate. When your answer is a guess or an estimate, you should tell me that you're guessing or giving an estimate. Will you agree to tell me when your answer is a guess or an estimate?

20. A: All right.

21. Q: If you answer a question and don't tell me that you are guessing at the answer, I'll assume that you are not guessing. Will that be a fair assumption on my part?

22. A: Yes.

23. Q: After you have answered a question, you may realize that for one reason or another you need to change an answer that you have previously given. If this happens, just tell me that you need to change an earlier answer and I'll give you an opportunity to do so. If you want to change an answer to an earlier question, will you tell me that you want to do so?

24. A: Yes.

25. Q: Also, after you've given your best complete answer to a question, you may sometimes later in the deposition remember additional information that responds to the question. If this happens, just tell me that you've remembered additional information that relates to an earlier question and you can tell me about the additional information. If after you have answered a question, you recall additional information will you tell me that?

26. A: Yes.

27. Q: If you find yourself getting tired at any time during the deposition, please let me know and we'll talk about taking a break. Is that all right?

28. A: That's fine.

29. Q: After the deposition is over, the court reporter will prepare a written transcript of my questions and your answers. You may have an opportunity to review and sign the transcript under penalty of perjury. If you review your transcript you may change answers that you believe are inaccurate. You should know, however, that if you make changes in the sworn testimony in your transcript after you review it, I and other lawyers in the case will be entitled at trial to ask you why you've made changes in your sworn testimony and to point out to the judge or jury at trial that you made changes. Do you understand that?

30. A: Yes.

31. Q: So it's important today to give me your most complete answers to my questions and to avoid any need to make changes in your testimony. Do you understand that?

32. A: Yes.

33. Q: You should also know that if you testify at trial differently than you testify here today, the lawyers in this case may have an opportunity to ask you why there were changes in your sworn testimony. Do you understand that?

34. A: Yes.

35. Q: I'm going to ask you a few questions about how you're feeling today. I am not trying

to pry into your medical situation, but I need to make sure anyone reading the transcript of this deposition will understand that you are feeling fine and are able to testify today. Are you ill today?

36. A: No.

37. Q: Do you feel fine physically?

38. A: Yes.

39. Q: Are you under any medication?

40. A: No

41. Q: Are you currently under a doctor's care for any illness?

42. A: Not now.

43. Q: Have you had any alcohol today?

44. A: No.

45. Q: Is there anything at all preventing you in any way from giving accurate testimony today?

46. A: No.

47. Q: Do you have any questions about what we've covered so far?

48. A: No.

49. Q: Do you have any questions of any kind before I begin the questioning?

50. A: No.

Transcript Analysis

A Lawsuit Has Been Filed (No. 1)—Here, you introduce yourself and explain briefly why the deposition is taking place. A statement such as this reflects common courtesy and may help to put a deponent at ease.

Answer Audibly (No. 3) and Let Me Finish My Questions (No. 5)—These admonitions seek to make life easier for the court reporter and hopefully improve a transcript's accuracy.

Prior Deposition Experience (No. 7)—Evidence that a deponent has prior deposition experience can undercut a deponent's explanation that confusion about deposition procedures caused the deponent to give erroneous testimony. Moreover, knowing that a deponent has prior experience can also help you evaluate the likelihood that the deponent will try to "play games" with you, such as by interpreting questions narrowly so as to conceal information. Even if a deponent has been deposed previously, you would complete the admonitions. Before doing so, you might say something along the lines of, "I realize that you are familiar with what happens at deposition, but just to make sure that there is no confusion let me explain what will happen here today."

Testifying Under Penalty of Perjury (Nos. 9, 11 and 13)—The answer to No. 9 undermines potential explanations for changed testimony based on a deponent's claim, "I wasn't that careful at deposition because I didn't think that I was under oath or testifying under penalty of perjury." Nos. 11 and 13 reinforce the point by establishing that a deponent knew that deposition testimony was as important as trial testimony and that the deponent agreed to try to tell the "complete" truth.

<u>If You Don't Understand, Don't Answer</u> (Nos. 15 and 17)—These admonitions undermine potential explanations by a deponent that changes in testimony resulted from misunderstanding deposition questions.

<u>Tell Me When You're Guessing</u> (Nos. 19 and 21)—These admonitions focus on the situation in which a deponent tries to justify a subsequent change in testimony based upon a claim that what seemed to be a definite deposition answer was in reality only a guess or an estimate.

You may choose to omit admonitions such as Nos. 19 and 21 in an effort to prevent deponents from guessing. Indeed, you may prefer to give an admonition which asks deponents not to answer at all if their only answer would be a guess. This alternative form of admonition may strengthen your attack on a deponent who later tries to justify a change in testimony by claiming that a deposition answer was only a guess. A potential downside, however, is that discouraging deponents from guessing may prevent you from obtaining leads to other potential evidence.

For example, assume that you represent tenants who have sued the owner of an apartment building, claiming that the owner is a slumlord who deliberately refused to make repairs. The deponent is a city building inspector who mailed a written Order to Comply to the owner requiring the owner to make listed repairs. You ask the inspector whether the owner ever considered making the repairs. If your admonitions have invited the inspector to guess, the inspector may respond by testifying, "I don't know, but my guess is that he didn't." You might then ask follow-up questions such as:

Q: What is the basis for your guess about whether the owner considered making the repairs listed in the Order?

Q: Why do you believe that the owner considered making the repairs listed in the Order?

Questions such as these might produce a helpful response such as, "Later on, a plumbing subcontractor told me that the owner had complained about the cost of redoing all the pipes in the apartment house." You might then follow up with the plumbing subcontractor to develop further evidence of the owner's neglect of the building. Had you admonished the deponent not to guess, the information may not have emerged.

<u>Changing an Answer</u> (No. 23)—This admonition undermines a post-deposition explanation for

changed testimony that runs along the lines of, "I would have provided the changed testimony during the deposition if I had known that I could change an incorrect answer during the deposition."

Again, you may prefer to omit an admonition similar to No. 23, in the belief that such an admonition may encourage a deponent to re-think helpful answers. Or, you may give an admonition along the lines of No. 23, but not until near a deposition's end. An admonition asking deponents whether they want to change answers already given may more strongly undermine post-deposition changes than a pre-questioning admonition such as No. 23. That is, a deponent may credibly be able to claim that "By the time we got to that answer, I'd forgotten that the attorney told me that I could change my answers during the deposition." On the other hand, that excuse has little credibility when you give the admonition just before a deposition concludes.

<u>Additional Information</u> (No. 25)—This admonition tends to encourage deponents to give complete responses. It recognizes that especially under the stress of a deposition, even the most forthcoming deponent will not always be able to remember all the information that responds to a question immediately after the question is asked. The admonition also makes it difficult for deponents to explain subsequent changes in deposition testimony by saying something like,

"I didn't think of the additional information until later on in the deposition, and by that time it was too late to mention it because we were on a whole different topic."

Taking a Break (No. 27)—This admonition tends to undermine an explanation for changed testimony along the lines of "When I gave that testimony at deposition, I was tired and not thinking clearly." Note that the question does not indicate that the deponent can take a break on demand. If you want a deponent to answer a question without consulting with opposing counsel, you may not want to immediately honor a request for a break. However, delaying a break will be more difficult if you commit at the outset to allowing deponents to take a break on demand.

Effect of Changed Deposition Testimony (Nos. 29, 31 and 33)—These admonitions encourage complete answers. They also diminish the likelihood that a deponent who changes an answer can effectively explain away the change by testifying, "I didn't think it was important to testify correctly during the deposition because I knew I'd have a chance to correct misstatements or omissions when I got the deposition transcript."

Mental and Physical Health (Nos. 35–45)—These admonitions undermine explanations along the lines of, "My deposition testimony was inaccurate (or, I couldn't remember very much) because I was ill (or, taking medication) on the day I was deposed."

If answers reveal that a deponent is ill, is taking medication or is under the influence of alcohol or other drugs, inquire into the nature of the illness, or the effects of the medications and drugs. If you're going to continue with the deposition, the record should reflect the deponent's acknowledgement that the deponent can testify fully and recall accurately notwithstanding the illness or medications. If you cannot secure such an acknowledgement, you may decide to postpone a deposition to a later date when the deponent may be better able to testify, stating for the record that the deponent's condition is the reason for the postponement.

<u>Any Questions</u> (Nos. 47 and 49)—These admonitions cut off justifications for changes of testimony based a deponent's lack of understanding of your admonitions or your failure to give a deponent a chance to ask about an important concern that your admonitions failed to cover.

If you refer back to the admonitions, you'll notice that following many of them, the lawyer asks the deponent to explicitly agree that the deponent understands what the lawyer has said. For example, in No. 1 the lawyer asks the deponent to affirm the deponent's understanding that the oral dialogue will become a written deposition transcript. By placing deponent's understanding explicitly on the record, you make it difficult for deponents to explain changes in testimony by saying, "I didn't understand the admonition in the first place."

C. QUESTIONS REGARDING A DEPONENT'S PREPARATION

After the admonitions, the next phase of depositions commonly concerns what a deponent did to prepare for a deposition. This section describes two common areas of inquiry relating to a deponent's preparation. Although most deponents prepare for a deposition by reviewing documents and speaking with counsel, you will want to find out everything that the witness did to prepare. It is often helpful to start this part of the deposition by asking: "Tell me everything you did to prepare for today's deposition."

1. Documents a Deponent Used to Refresh Recollection

1. Q: Ms. Jones did you review any documents when you were preparing for your deposition?

2. A: Yes.

3. Q: Reviewing those documents helped to refresh your memory about some of the facts of this case, is that correct?

4. A: I suppose that's true.

5. Q: Could you please identify for me the documents you reviewed to prepare for your deposition?

6. Opposing Counsel: I think I can speed this up. This folder contains all the documents my client reviewed in preparation for testifying here today.

7. Q: I am showing you documents from the folder that your lawyer just gave me. The court reporter has marked these documents as Exhibits 750 through 810. Can you look at them please and tell me if these are the documents you reviewed in preparation for your deposition?

8. A: Yes, these are the documents I looked at.

9. Q: Did you review any other documents in preparation for your deposition?

10. A: No, just these.

FRE 612 provides that if, prior to testifying, witnesses use a writing to refresh their memory for the purpose of testifying, adverse parties are generally entitled to have the writings produced at the hearing. While FRE 612 pertains to testimony at trial, the rule also generally applies to testimony at deposition.

To use FRE 612 to gain access to documents which you may not have previously seen, at the outset of depositions ask deponents to identify the documents they reviewed to prepare for deposition, and whether those documents refreshed their memory about the facts of a case. Often, as above, opposing counsel will willingly provide such documents at deposition. Doing so speeds up depositions and may eliminate the need for additional sessions to examine deponents regarding documents that you are entitled to see but were not provided with at deposition. Also as above, ask deponents if they reviewed any documents besides those provided to you by opposing counsel.

Opposing counsel may object to the production of some or all of the documents used to refresh a deponent's recollection, usually on the grounds of attorney-client or work product privilege. This objection may be raised on the ground that documents themselves constitute attorney work product or refer to attorney-client communications. Alternatively, the privilege claim may rest on the ground that the selection of documents used to refresh recollection might itself reveal opposing counsel's analysis of legal or factual issues. If opposing counsel refuses to produce the documents, you typically go forward with your questioning without them and then decide whether you want to adjourn the deposition and move for an order compelling their production. At the hearing on the motion, the court decides whether the interests of justice require production of the documents. If the order is granted and the documents are turned over, you can then complete the deposition.

When opposing counsel refuses at deposition to provide documents used by a deponent to refresh recollection on the ground that the selection of those documents is likely to reveal opposing counsel's analysis of legal or factual issues, you may still be able to identify and gain access to some of those documents during the deposition itself. To do so, follow up a deponent's answer with a question such as:

> Q: "Are you aware of any document which you believe supports the testimony that you have just given?"

If the answer is "yes," you might be entitled to ask for and obtain a copy of the document. Since furnishing the document in these circumstances doesn't reveal opposing counsel's selection of documents, the work product claim probably will not in this scenario block your access to a document.

2. Persons with Whom a Deponent Talked

Just as you should ask about documents a deponent may have reviewed, so too should you ask about persons a deponent may have talked to in preparation for the deposition. Conversations with persons other than the deponent's attorney may not be privileged. If so, you can examine the deponent (as well as the other persons) about the reasons for and what was said during any and all such conversations.

D. BACKGROUND QUESTIONING

A final common beginning phase of depositions concerns deponents' backgrounds. Background questions typically probe deponents' educational and employment history. Many lawyers ask "background" questions simply because they have seen other lawyers do it, without really knowing why they are asking such questions or what they are looking for. As a result, background questioning is often nothing more than a chance for a questioning attorney to "warm up" and try to build rapport with a deponent. While these goals are themselves of value, background questioning may also serve more valuable functions. For example, knowing a deponent's background may help you to identify areas where the deponent's subsequent testimony seems inconsistent with prior experience. In addition, you can sometimes obscure the significance of important inquiries by asking them in seemingly insignificant background questioning.

1. Employment History

A useful approach for eliciting testimony concerning a deponent's employment history is to obtain a timeline. Your timeline may either begin with a deponent's most recent employment and move backwards, or begin at an earlier time and move forward to the present.

Employment-related questioning may uncover evidence bearing on a deponent's personal credibility. For example, a deponent who testifies on behalf of a party who formerly employed the deponent is more susceptible to a claim of bias if the deponent worked for the party for twenty years than if the deponent worked for the party for two years. Of course, the conclusion may be the opposite if the deponent worked for a party for twenty years and was terminated six months before the deponent's pension vested! For that reason, it may be important to find out not only the sequence of a deponent's past jobs, but also the circumstances under which the deponent left each job.

Employment-related questioning may also uncover evidence bearing on the reliability of a deponent's observations. For example, if a deponent testifies to an opinion that a driver involved in a lawsuit appeared to be under the influence of alcohol, evidence that the deponent worked as a part-time bartender during college tends to increase the reliability of the opinion. Similarly, if the supervisor of a plaintiff in a wrongful termination case testifies that the plaintiff was one of the least capable employees the supervisor had ever worked with, the reliability of the supervisor's assertion may depend on how many employees the supervisor has worked with and over how long a period of time.

2. Educational Background

A timeline of a deponent's educational background also may help you to evaluate both a deponent's credibility and the reliability of a deponent's testimony. For example, assume that you depose the defendant in a Clean Water Act case in which the magnitude of the penalty imposed for a violation depends in part on whether the defendant acted in good faith. The defendant claims ignorance of applicable environmental regulations. Evidence that the deponent had taken courses covering environmental regulations in the deponent's industry would tend to undermine this claim. Similarly, in a real estate fraud case in which the plaintiff must prove reasonable reliance on a defendant's misrepresentations, evidence concerning the plaintiff's educational background might affect the likelihood or the reasonableness of the plaintiff's reliance on the defendant's misstatements.

E. PRIOR EXPERIENCE TESTIFYING AT A DEPOSITION OR TRIAL

For at least two reasons it can often be helpful to find out about a deponent's prior experience testifying at a deposition or trial. First, it can provide you with a sense of how knowledgeable and/or comfortable the deponent is with the deposition process. Second, it can allow you to find out if the deponent has ever testified in a case that involved facts or issues similar to your case. For example, if you are deposing the Human Resources manager of the defendant in an age discrimination case, you will want to find out if the manager testified in other cases involving age discrimination. If so, you may want to obtain access to transcripts of the manager's prior depositions to see if they contain information that is helpful to your case or provides a basis for impeaching the manager's testimony in your case.

2. CONCLUDING DEPOSITIONS

Just before concluding your questioning, you may choose to ask questions such as:

> "Are all of the answers you've given in this deposition complete and accurate?"
>
> "Do you want to change any of the answers you've given in this deposition?"

"Do you want to add to any of the answers you've given in this deposition?"

Such questions are likely to enhance impeachment should a deponent make a change in deposition testimony or later give testimony that conflicts with deposition testimony. The possible downside of such questions is that they may encourage a deponent to change helpful answers.

After you have finished your questions, lawyers representing all other parties are entitled to question the deponent. Not surprisingly, deposition questioning typically ends when each party's lawyer says something like, "I have no further questions." At that point, any party or a deponent may request that the deponent have an opportunity to read and sign the deposition transcript. In the absence of such a request, a deponent has no right to review and correct a deposition transcript. The court reporter will prepare and certify the deposition transcript and send it to you as the deposing attorney. You should retain the transcript unless and until it is needed later in a case.

If any party or a deponent asks that the deponent have an opportunity to read and sign the deposition transcript, the court reporter prepares a transcript and notifies a deponent that the deponent has thirty days to review and sign the transcript. After receiving the notice, the deponent normally goes to the court reporter's place of business and may make any changes in the transcript that the deponent deems necessary. Simultaneously, the deponent should prepare a separate document indicating the reasons for any changes. After the transcript review is complete and the deponent has signed the transcript, the court reporter certifies the transcript, including any changes and reasons for any changes, and sends the transcript to you to retain unless and until it is needed later in a case.

Through stipulations, attorneys often substitute their own signing procedures for those set forth in the FRCP. For example, a common stipulation relieves deponents of the obligation to go to court reporters' offices in order to review deposition transcripts and instead allows the review to take place at the office of the deponent's attorney. However, stipulations tend to vary according to local customs and practice areas. At the end of the day, do not agree to a stipulation unless you fully understand its effect.

CHAPTER 5

TIMELINE QUESTIONING

Timelines are chronologically-ordered series of events. Timeline questioning aimed at developing a chronology helps you accomplish a number of important deposition goals.

- Stories necessarily consist of events that unfold over time. As a wit once observed, without time everything would happen all at once. Thus, timeline questioning helps you understand deponents' stories.

- The order of events affects the inferences that flow from them.

  Example: "Harry left the office, drove down Third Ave., swerved into a telephone pole, went into a bar, and had two martinis" versus "Harry left the office, went into a bar, had two martinis, drove down Third Ave., and swerved into a telephone pole."

- Timeline questioning promotes thoroughness. When you pursue timelines, deponents may identify events that you did not know about. This is particularly important when a deponent participated in events that your client was unaware of, such as an anti-trust case in which the deponent participated in meetings with competitors to fix prices.

- As testimony typically emerges chronologically at trial, timeline questioning aids trial preparation by serving as a preview of a deponent's direct examination testimony. The preview helps you assess and prepare to undermine its credibility.

1. TIMELINE QUESTIONING BASICS

This section provides a template format for pursuing a chronological version of a deponent's story.

- **Styles of Questions**

Effective timeline questioning generally involves a mixture of open and closed or leading questions. Open questions encourage deponents to discuss events in order from their own memories, while closed questions allow you to search thoroughly for additional events. Closed and leading questions can also be used to obtain more detail about events identified by the deponent.

- **Choose a Timeline Definition**

Before you ask your first timeline question, you need to define your timeline. If you simply ask a deponent, "What happened first?" your question may well be met with a "vague" objection. To avoid having your questioning derailed by potentially valid objections (which are discussed in more detail in Chapter 12) provide a deponent with a timeline definition that identifies the topic you wish to explore. For example, if you want a deponent to provide a chronology relating to a potential tenant's interest in an apartment, instead of asking "What happened first?" you could ask, "When was the first time that you learned that Ms. Hsu might be interested in the apartment?" Incorporating the details of your timeline definition into your timeline questions provides clarity on the topic you wish to explore as well as avoids objections.

- **Seek the Earliest Timeline Event**

In Rodgers and Hammerstein's musical play *The Sound of Music* Maria sings, "Let's start at the very beginning, a very good place to start." Maria is teaching children how to create a song, but she might just as well have been teaching lawyers how to develop timelines. The first dispute-related event in a deponent's story is indeed a very good place to start. But as an ancient text advises, "All beginnings are hard." You may be uncertain about whether you have obtained a story's "true" beginning.

Timeline questioning normally begins with an attempt to identify the first event that occurred within your timeline definition. For example, you could ask the straightforward open question mentioned above, "When was the first time that you learned that Ms. Hsu might be interested in the apartment?"

Assume the deponent responds, "I received Ms. Hsu's written application in May and then I talked about it with Mark, the other manager in the office."

The deponent's answer at least implicitly identifies the first event of your timeline definition and implies that nothing happened prior to the receipt of the application in May. But to confirm whether this is really the first event in the timeline you should gap check backwards. For example, you might follow up with:

Q: Just to make sure we're on the same page, prior to receiving the application in May, did anything happen that indicated Ms. Hsu might be interested in the apartment?

A: Well, my supervisor told me that we might receive an application from Ms. Hsu about a week before it showed up in my Inbox.

The deponent's answer to your gap check question reveals an earlier start to the timeline. To be certain this newly-identified event was the first event, you might again gap check backwards to make sure no earlier events took place. Once you are confident that an event is the first event within your timeline definition, you are ready to move forward.

- **Move a Timeline Forward**

You typically move forward from the first event in a timeline with open "next event" questions. Here, you might ask one of the following questions:

Q: After your supervisor told you that you might receive an application from Ms. Hsu, what was the next thing that happened relating to her interest in the property?

Q: After you received the application from Ms. Hsu in May, what was the next thing that happened relating to her interest in the property?

Q: After you spoke to Mark about Ms. Hsu's application, what was the next thing that happened relating to her interest in the property?

- **Dates, Approximations and Intervals**

As you move a timeline forward, to the extent possible try to clarify it by obtaining events' dates, or at least the approximate times or dates of events and the intervals between them. For example:

Q: Do you recall when your supervisor told you that you might receive an application from Ms. Hsu?

Q: Do you recall when in May you received the application from Ms. Hsu?

Q: How long after you received Ms. Hsu's application did you discuss it with Mark?

- **Check for Gaps**

When you suspect (perhaps based on information already reported to you) that a deponent may have skipped over an important event, you may seek to fill in possible gaps by asking open and/or closed questions that seek to identify events that may have taken place between the events a deponent has already disclosed. For example:

Q: Between the time you first heard that Ms. Hsu might be submitting an application and when you received her application in May, did anything else happen that in any way relates to her application?

Q: Between the time you first heard that Ms. Hsu might be submitting an application and when you received her application in May, did you discuss Ms. Hsu with your supervisor?

Q: Between the time you first heard that Ms. Hsu might be submitting an application and when you received her application in May, did you conduct a background check on Ms. Hsu?

You may unwittingly create a gap if you mistakenly assume that an event testified to by a deponent is the "very next thing that happened." For example, assume that the following testimony unfolds:

Q: What happened next regarding Ms. Hsu's application?

A: Mark and I discussed her application. We had some concerns about her ability to pay so we talked to my supervisor and the supervisor suggested that we run a credit check. It was a few days before I noticed the credit check came in and after it came in, Mark and I met again to discuss whether we should rent to Ms. Hsu.

Q: What happened when you and Mark met again to discuss whether to rent to Ms. Hsu?

Here, when the deponent refers to a future event (a meeting with Mark), the questioner immediately inquires about it. But this later meeting to discuss whether to rent to Ms. Hsu may not in fact have been the next relevant event.

To avoid skipping over potentially important events, you may want to gap check:

> Q: Just so I'm clear, did anything related to Ms. Hsu's application take place between when you ran a credit check and when you met again with Mark after the credit check came in?

- **The End?**

When deponents seemingly have finished timeline stories, you may as a matter of course ask about possible later events. Your questions may be open if you have no reason to suspect that later events took place, or closed if you think (even if only based on experience) that later events were likely. For example:

> Q: After you orally informed Ms. Hsu that she was not financially qualified to rent the apartment, what was the next thing that happened?
>
> A: We were served with a complaint alleging that we illegally refused to rent to her. That's when we contacted our lawyer.

The answer suggests that the deponent has finished with the timeline. But you may check for possible later events with open and/or closed questions. For example:

> Q: Before you contacted your lawyer did anything else related to Ms. Hsu take place?

Q: Before you contacted your lawyer, were you contacted by anyone from the city's fair housing department?

2. AN ILLUSTRATIVE EXAMPLE

The following example illustrates timeline questioning.

1. Q: You said earlier in your testimony that at some point you began to feel that you were being forced out. When did you first feel that you were being forced out?

2. A: When I learned that Smith was being placed in charge of the outside sales force.

3. Q: When did you learn about this?

4. A: When I had a meeting with Harold and Arlene.

5. Q: When was that meeting?

6. A: It was in the afternoon, sometime in early September.

7. Q: Okay. After the meeting with Harold and Arlene when you were told that Smith was being placed in charge of the outside sales force, what was the next thing that happened that led you to think you were being forced out?

8. A: About two weeks later, I got a call from Arthur Rosett telling me that productivity in my department was not what it might be and that he'd like to discuss some changes that might help increase production.

9. Q: Between the time of the meeting with Harold and Arlene and the call from Rosett, did anything else happen that led you to think you were being forced out?

10. A: No.

11. Q: Between the time of the meeting with Harold and Arlene and the call from Rosett, did you receive any messages from anyone that led you to think you were being forced out?

12. A: No.

13. Q: After the call from Rosett, what was the next thing that led you to believe that you were being forced out?

14. A: I didn't receive a discretionary bonus at the end of the year.

15. Q: Between the time you got the call from Rosett and the failure to receive a discretionary bonus at the end of the year, did anything else happen that led you to think that you were being forced out?

16. A: No.

17. Q: What was the next thing that happened after the failure to receive a bonus at the end of the year that led you to think you were being forced out?

18. A: Well. . .

In this example, the first question identifies the timeline definition, the deponent's feeling of being forced out, and asks for the first event. Questions 3 and 5 identify the approximate time when a particular event took place. Questions 7, 13 and 17 move the timeline forward to the next event, while Questions 9, 11 and 15 check for gaps.

3. OVERCOMING COMMON TIMELINE CHALLENGES

This section addresses common challenges to eliciting effective timelines.

A. PROBLEM: A DEPONENT CANNOT ORGANIZE IMPORTANT EVENTS CHRONOLOGICALLY

Deponents may be unable, or claim to be unable, to remember the chronological order in which important events occurred. In such situations, you may abandon the timeline questioning pattern and instead probe topics through T-funnel questioning without regard to the order in which events related to those topics took place. Chapter 6 illustrates this strategy.

B. PROBLEM: OVERLY-BROAD TOPICS

Timeline questioning is more likely to be productive and helpful for evaluating the strength of your legal claims if you focus deponents on discrete topics. Overly broad, vague subjects such as, "Please tell me everything you can about people's existential search for meaning," are unlikely to be productive. In the rhetorical as well as the physical world, the postulate "the angle of incidence equals the angle of reflection" generally means that vague questions produce vague answers.

For example, assume that you represent the plaintiff in a wrongful termination case in which the defendant deponent claims that your client's actions constituted just cause for termination. You start timeline questioning with, "Please tell me the first thing about my client's employment history." The topic "employment history" is too vague to produce a meaningful timeline.

A more effective approach would be to ask about the types of behaviors that allegedly constituted just cause for termination. You might then seek to elicit separate timelines for each type of behavior. Assume the deponent testifies, "One problem was that your client dropped the ball on the Prager account." You might then start timeline questioning on this discrete topic by asking, "When did you first become aware of a problem with the Prager account."

C. PROBLEM: OVERLY-BROAD RESPONSES

Daily experience often fails to equip non-professional witnesses with the discipline to proceed chronologically through a series of discrete events.

Example:

Q: When did you first become aware that a car was approaching the intersection at a high rate of speed?

A: I had seen the kids in the crosswalk, one was wearing inline skates. I could tell from the

> sound that a car was quickly accelerating in the direction of the crosswalk. It was terrifying. It seemed like it was just a few seconds before the car hit the kids.

To elicit a timeline in a situation like this, you can advise a deponent that you want to go through the story event-by-event. In the above example, you might follow the answer with a comment along these lines:

> I want to find out everything you can tell me about what happened. But I'd like you to go step-by-step through everything you can remember hearing and seeing that night. I understand that you may not be exact, just do the best you can. Will you try to do that? OK, so please start by telling me just the first thing you can remember about what happened that night.

Depending on the circumstances, you may have to make similar admonitions a few times during a deposition.

D. PROBLEM: SIDE-TRACKING

A deponent may mention an event that is not related to the timeline you are pursuing. When this happens you may be tempted to pounce on the unrelated event immediately. You may think, "I'll just ask a question or two and then get back to my timeline." The risk is that you stray farther from the timeline topic than you intended, and you neglect to complete the initial timeline. Thus, even if an unrelated event seems important, usually you should "park" it. Finish your initial timeline, then return to the parked event when it makes sense to do so. You may tell a deponent, "I'll want to ask you about that later in the deposition. For the moment, let's go back to. . ."

CHAPTER 6

T-FUNNEL QUESTIONING

T-Funnel questioning is a strategy for thoroughly probing topics and events that occur inside adverse deponents' timeline stories. By integrating T-Funnel questions with timeline questioning (see Chapter 5), you encourage witnesses to describe events in their own words while you probe for evidence that helps you:

- Prepare for settlement and trial by pinning deponents to their stories;
- Uncover harmful testimony and seek to undermine its probative value and credibility; and
- Identify helpful evidence and bolster its probative value and credibility.

Generally, timeline and T-Funnel questioning go on simultaneously. That is, you move back and forth between pursuing a sequential order of events and searching for more information about important events with T-Funnel sequences. However, you may instead choose to pursue surface-level timeline questioning that seeks to identify the order of important events without pausing to explore the details of discrete events. Since most depositions are limited to a single day of questioning, surface-level timelines can help you decide which events to circle back to and probe with T-Funnel questioning. For example, if you have only very limited knowledge of a deponent's story, you may want to first elicit a surface-level timeline before deciding which events are most important to probe thoroughly with T-Funnel questioning.

1. THE T-FUNNEL QUESTIONING PATTERN

T-Funnel questioning combines two basic memory-stimulating components:

- The horizontal top of the "T" consists of open or narrative questions that encourage witnesses to describe topics or events in their own words. "Free recall" story-telling that relies on witnesses' paths of association may surface important information that you would not have thought to ask about.
- The vertical stem of the "T" consists of closed or leading questions that search for details that can help you analyze the extent of harmful evidence or a witness' ability to provide helpful evidence that advances your legal claims.

To utilize a T-Funnel, you ask a series of open questions about a subject until the deponent indicates that there is nothing else responsive to that topic. Then you further explore the subject by asking closed or leading questions about that same topic in an attempt to uncover information the deponent failed to volunteer in response to open questions. Visually, the T-Funnel pattern looks like this:

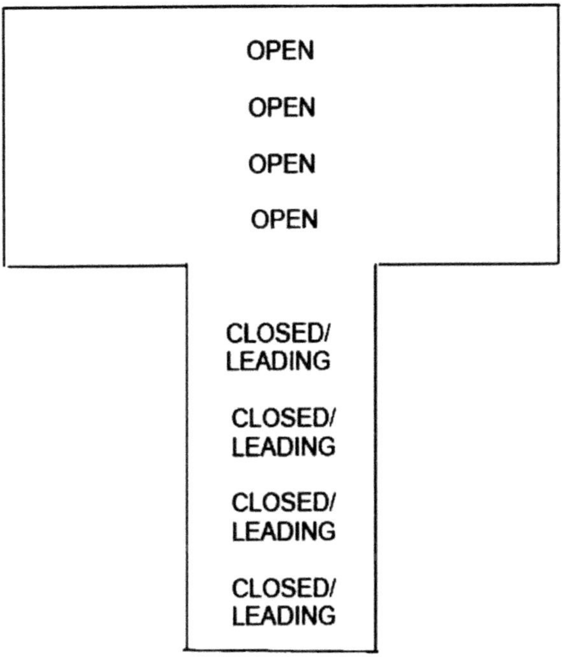

A. AN ILLUSTRATION OF THE T-FUNNEL PATTERN

The following sequence illustrates how you may use T-Funnel questioning to probe the topic "people who reported directly to the deponent."

1. Q: Who are the people that reported directly to you?

2. A: Paul Blasi, Jack Carlson and Ann Freeman.

3. Q: Who else reported directly to you?

4. A: Well, I guess you could say that Dave Moore did also.

5. Q: Who else reported to you?

6. A: That's it; just those four people.

7. Q: Miguel Perice reported to you, didn't he?

8. A: Yes, sometimes he reported to me.

9. Q: How about Melinda Johnson, did she report to you?

10. A: No, she did not report directly to me.

11. Q: Shari Binder reported to you as well, correct?

12. A: Once in a while she reported to me, yes.

13. Q: Have you now told me about everyone who reported to you?

14. A: Yes.

In this example, you begin with open questions (Nos. 1, 3 and 5). These questions are "open" because you allow the witness to decide on the content and scope of the answers.

Then, when the open questions appear to have exhausted the deponent's independent recollection (No. 6), you turn to closed/leading questions (Nos. 7, 9, 11 and 13) seeking additional information that the deponent may have omitted. Closed questions typically seek a "yes" or "no" answer (Nos. 9 and 13).

Leading questions are closed questions that suggest the desired "yes" or "no" answer (Nos. 7 and 11).[1]

As this example suggests, T-Funnel questioning is a particularly helpful way to get the deponent to provide you with a complete list: e.g. everyone who attended a meeting; all of the reasons why the deponent fired your client. Ensuring that the deponent is providing you with a complete list is important for at least two reasons. First, in ordinary conversation, people will often only provide one or two items in a list. Second, some deponents will attempt to conceal information that is harmful to them by providing only a partial list that leaves out the harmful information. The T-Funnel technique—particularly if you consistently end sequences by getting deponents to confirm that they have provided you with complete information—can minimize that risk.

Effective deposition preparation includes thinking about fruitful subjects for the stem sections of T-Funnel questioning. Try to identify specific items of helpful evidence that a witness might be able to provide. Deciding whether to ask closed/leading questions to ferret out the extent of the damaging information that a deponent may be able to provide is a strategic judgment. But you can advance your legal claims if you can show that a deponent is unable to provide damaging information. And if a question uncovers damaging information, you are better able to respond if you uncover the information at

---

[1] At a deposition of an adverse witness, you are entitled to ask closed/leading questions at any time. See FRE 611(c).

deposition rather than find out about it during settlement negotiations or at trial.

B. USING A SERIES OF T-FUNNELS

Any information that a witness provides in response to T-Funnel questioning can serve as the basis of a new and secondary T-Funnel sequence. When events or topics are sufficiently important, deposition questioning can consist of a series of T-Funnel sequences.

> Example: You represent the plaintiff in a wrongful termination case and are deposing your client's former supervisor. You seek the deponent's version of what happened at an important meeting when the deponent and your client reviewed your client's last performance report.

Initial T-Funnel—Top of the T Questions

1. Q: Mr. Gillig, you said that you met with my client on March 2 to review his last performance report. Please tell me everything you can recall about that meeting.

2. A: Well, we discussed the contents of the report and I told him that he'd have to improve.

3. Q: Other than going over the report, and telling him he'd have to improve, what else happened?

4. A: Nothing.

Initial T-Funnel—Stem of the T Questions

5. Q: Did you discuss any documents other than his performance report during that meeting?

6. A: Yes, we briefly went over the written response that he had made to the performance report.

7. Q: Did you discuss any other documents?

8. A: No.

9. Q: Did you talk about what might happen if my client did not improve during that March 2 meeting?

10. A: Yes, we did discuss that.

11. Q: Okay, and you talked about a timetable for evaluating my client's performance, correct?

12. A: Yes. I told him that I'd be giving him another review in a month.

13. Q: Did you talk about any changes in my client's responsibilities during that meeting?

14. A: No, we didn't talk about that.

15. Q: Did you discuss anything else at the meeting other than what you have told me about?

16. A: No.

During this initial T-Funnel questioning, using both open questions at the top of the T and closed/leading questions at the stem of the T, you identified the following topics that were discussed at a meeting:

(1) The contents of the performance report.

(2) The need for your client to improve.

(3) Your client's written response to the performance report.

(4) What might happen if your client did not improve.

(5) A timetable for evaluating your client's performance.

You could use Secondary T-Funnel questioning to probe any of these topics you think might be important. For example, Secondary T-Funnel questioning of Topic (1) above might begin as follows:

<u>Secondary T-Funnel #1—Top of the T Questions</u>

21. Q: I'm showing you what has been marked as Exhibit 27. Is this the performance report you went over with my client during the March 2nd meeting?

22. A: Yes.

23. Q: Please tell me everything you recall about the discussion of the performance report.

24. . . . .

25. Q: What else do you remember saying about the performance report?

26. A: That's all we discussed.

Secondary T-Funnel #1—Stem of the T Questions

27. Q: Did you tell my client his attitude was unsatisfactory when you discussed his performance report?

28. A: Not exactly.

29. Q: And you didn't tell my client that he had a problem reporting to work on time when you discussed his performance review, correct?

30. A: That's accurate.

31. Q: Did you identify the departments that provided the information on which you based the performance report when you talked to my client about the report?

32. A: No. . . .

After completing this Secondary T-Funnel, you could then utilize Secondary T-Funnels to explore any or all of the other topics identified in response to the initial T-Funnel—what was discussed about the need for your client to improve, the client's written response to the report, what might happen if he did not improve, and the timetable for evaluating performance.

The extent of T-Funnel questioning for any event or topic is a matter of judgment. Naturally, the more significant a topic or event, the more extensively you are likely to pursue it. In theory the process of using information that emerges in the course of one T-Funnel sequence as the basis of a secondary T-Funnel sequence can continue indefinitely, like images in mirrors that face each other. In practice, factors such as deposition time limits and limits on human memory ability mean that you will move on to new events and topics long before you get to the vanishing point.

2. "PARKING" SUBJECTS FOR LATER INQUIRY

In the course of T-Funnel questioning, a deponent may mention information that is important but not necessarily related to the subject of the T-Funnel sequence. The temptation is to abandon the subject you were T-Funneling and pursue the new information at once. Most of the time the better choice is to resist the temptation. Park the new information to the side, finish the T-Funnel that you have already started, and later pursue the new information.

To minimize the risk that you will forget to go back and do follow-up questioning about the "parked" information, it is helpful to use a system of taking notes that will flag for you the need to do further questioning.

3. INVERTED T-FUNNELS

Another way to use a T-Funnel pattern is to turn it upside down and ask closed/leading questions first, followed by open questions. This pattern may work better than the normal T-Funnel pattern because it avoids people's psychological tendencies to conform specific data to previously-expressed opinions.

In a child custody case for example you might use an inverted T-Funnel to help you surface information indicating that your client was a good father. For example:

1. Q: Did you ever see Mr. Yeazell help his children with their homework?

2. A: No.

3. Q: Did you ever see Mr. Yeazell cook dinner for the children?

4. A: A couple of times.

5. Q: Do you know if Mr. Yeazell ever took his children to sporting events?

6. A: Yes. He took them to soccer games and baseball games.

7. Q: Did you ever see him playing games on iPads with his children?

8. A: Sure, but he would often put strict limits on how long they could spend on electronic games.

9. Q: And you often saw Mr. Yeazell put the children to bed, correct?

10. A: Yes.

11. Q: Tell me about any other things you observed that you thought were positive

interactions between Mr. Yeazell and his children.

12. A: Well he would sometimes. . .

In this example, you invert the T-funnel by asking closed/leading questions first (Questions 1–9) and following up with an open question (Question 11) to find out about helpful information your closed questions may have missed. Had you begun by asking the deponent for an opinion (e.g. "Did you ever see Mr. Yeazell have what you thought were positive interactions with his children?") and the adverse deponent gives a negative answer, the deponent may then have been inclined to conform answers to subsequent questions to the harmful opinion. The inverted T-Funnel seeks to avoid the potential biasing effect of asking for the opinion first.

4. COMMON T-FUNNELS

The subjects of T-Funnel questioning obviously depend on the legal and factual issues in individual cases. This section illustrates common T-Funnel questioning sequences.

A. "EVERYTHING THAT HAPPENED" T-FUNNELS

Perhaps the most common use of T-Funnels or a series of T-Funnel sequences is to learn what happened on a specific occasion.

Example 1

"Tell me everything that occurred during the meeting in Mr. Hobbs' office."

"What else occurred during that meeting?"

> "Did X occur?"
>
> "Did Y occur?"

Example 2

"Tell me everything that occurred from the time the police arrived until the ambulance got there."

"What else happened during that window of time?

> "Did X occur?"
>
> "Did Y occur?"

"Event Essentials"

When using T-Funnels to explore what happened during events, you will also often want to get "Event Essentials" such as: (1) who was present at the event; (2) where was the event; (3) when the event took place; (4) how long the event lasted; (5) why the event took place; and (6) whether a written or electronic record of the event exists. While these questions may not necessarily fit inside of the T-Funnel, they can provide helpful information and constitute foundational evidence that advances admissibility at trial. You may seek event essentials either before or after your T-Funnel questioning.

B. "EVERYTHING YOU DID OR SAID" T-FUNNELS

You may use T-Funnels to investigate all that a deponent did or said.

Example 1

"Tell me everything that you did to investigate my client's claim that she was being treated unfairly."

"What else did you do to investigate the claim?"

"Did you. . .?"

"Did you. . .?"

Example 2

"Tell me everything that you did to try to obtain construction financing between the time of the initial meeting and the meeting on the fourth of February."

"What else did you do to try to obtain financing?"

"Did you. . .?"

"Did you. . .?"

Example 3

"Tell me everything you told Ms. Jones about the stock before she agreed to purchase the 2500 shares."

"What else did you tell her?"

"Did you. . .?"

"Did you. . .?"

C. "ALL THE REASONS" T-FUNNELS

You may use T-Funnel sequences to uncover all the reasons why a deponent acted or failed to act on a particular occasion.

Example 1

"Tell me all the reasons that you denied my client's request for a transfer to another department."

"What other reasons did you have to deny the request?"

"Was another reason. . .?"

"Was another reason. . .?"

Example 2

"Tell me all the reasons that you decided not to include the language on Exhibit 12 in the final report."

"Why else did you decide not to include that language?"

"Was another reason. . .?"

"Was another reason. . .?"

D. "BASIS FOR A CONCLUSION, OPINION OR BELIEF" T-FUNNELS

When a deponent testifies to an opinion, conclusion or belief regarding an important matter, you can use

T-Funnel questioning to uncover the bases for the conclusion, opinion or belief.

Example 1

"Please tell me all the reasons why you concluded that Mr. Grubb was not financially qualified."

"Were there any other reasons why you concluded he was not qualified?"

"Was another reason. . .?

"Was another reason. . .?

Example 2

"Please tell me everything you observed that led you to conclude the software program was defective."

"What else led you to conclude the program was defective?"

"Was another reason. . .?

"Was another reason. . .?

E. "HELPFUL INFORMATION" T-FUNNELS

Adverse witnesses may be able to provide information that supports your legal claims.

Example 1 (child custody case)

"Can you tell me about occasions on which my client demonstrated concern for the child?"

"Any other occasions you observed my client show concern for the child?

"Did you ever observe. . . .?"

"Did you ever observe. . . .?"

Example 2 (car accident case)

"Were there any circumstances that interfered with your ability to observe the speed of the car?"

"Any other circumstances that interfered with your ability to observe the speed of the car?"

"Did the weather interfere with your ability to observe the speed of the car?"

"Did intoxication interfere with your ability to observe the speed of the car?

5. EVENT BY EVENT QUESTIONING: COMBINING TIMELINES WITH T-FUNNELS

Timeline questioning helps you to produce a chronology of important events, and T-Funnel questioning expands the chronology into a detailed story by enabling you to uncover event details. Combining timeline and T-Funnel questioning helps you to obtain as complete a picture as possible of a deponent's version of significant events by using the following template:

(1) Ask for the first event in your timeline definition

(2) Gap check backwards to confirm no prior events took place

(3) Ask for Event Essentials

(4) Use T-Funnel questioning techniques to discover what happened at that event

(5) Use Secondary T-Funnels to explore any topics identified in response to your initial T-Funnel which you wish to probe further

(6) Ask for the next event in your timeline definition (and repeat this process until you reach the end of the chronology)

For example, assume that you represent the defendant in the case of *Terry v. Biderman Construction Co.* Biderman Construction built a concrete processing plant in the city of Lyte. Ann Terry, a homeowner living near the plant, has sued Biderman alleging that the plant is a nuisance and that Biderman made numerous misrepresentations to the Lyte City Council when applying for the permit to build the plant. The suit seeks compensatory and punitive damages for Biderman's knowing and willful maintenance of a nuisance and for intentional infliction of emotional distress. You are deposing plaintiff Terry.

You would undoubtedly have to develop a number of timelines to elicit Terry's complete version of significant events. For example, you would want to try to obtain timelines for misrepresentations allegedly made by the defendant to the City Council and the property damage suffered as a result of the operation of the plant. For illustrative purposes, the following example focuses on a single topic: complaints that Terry allegedly made about the plant.

1. Q: Ms. Terry, you mentioned earlier that you complained about the plant and what was going on there. So I'd like to ask you about any complaints you made to anyone in any way related to the plant. If possible, I'd like to start at the beginning and go through each complaint one by one. Could you tell me when was the first time you complained to someone about the plant?

[Question 1 seeks the first event within the timeline definition]

2. A: Do you want to know about the complaints I made to the people at the city or the times I called Biderman and told him about the problems?

3. Q: I want to know about both. In fact, I want to know about any complaints you made to anyone: the people with the city, Mr. Biderman or anyone else. So when was the first time that you made a complaint to anyone that related to the plant?

4. A: I don't remember the exact date but the first time was when I called my councilman, Mr. Stevenson.

5. Q: Did you complain to anyone before calling Mr. Stevenson?

[Question 5 checks for gaps before the first event identified]

6. A: No

7. Q: Okay, I know it's hard to remember exact dates sometimes, but could you tell me approximately when you called Mr. Stevenson?

8. A: It was about a month or so after they opened that plant.

9. Q: How long was your call with Mr. Stevenson?

[Questions 7 and 9 probe for Event Essentials]

10. A: Maybe five minutes.

11. Q: All right, I'd like you to tell me everything that you can recall that you talked about with Mr. Stevenson when you first talked to him about the plant.

[Question 11 starts the T-Funnel with an open question about what happened during the first event, the complaint to Stevenson]

12. A: Well, I told him that there were trucks delivering stuff to the plant at all hours of the day and night and that the noise was too much, and they'd have to get them to stop taking deliveries and making so much noise, especially late at night because it was making it hard to sleep.

13. Q: Other than saying that the plant was making too much noise and taking deliveries at all hours of the night, did you say anything else to Mr. Stevenson in this first call?

14. A: That was pretty much it in the first call, because we hadn't started to have any problems with the dust at that time. So I was just complaining about the noise. But later, I called Stevenson two other times to complain about the dust and to complain about the noise again.

15. Q: For right now, I'd like to stick to the first call. We'll talk about what happened in the other calls later. Did you talk to Mr. Stevenson about anything other than the noise and taking deliveries at all hours of the night in that first call?

[Questions 13 and 15 continue the top of the T-funnel with open questions about what happened during the first event, the complaint to Stevenson.]

16. A: No, that was all in the first call.

17. Q: Did you tell Mr. Stevenson that other neighbors also felt that the plant was a nuisance during that initial call?

[Question 17 moves to the stem of the T-Funnel, asking a closed question about things that might have happened during that first event]

18. A: No.

19. Q: Now, I'd like you to tell me everything you and Mr. Stevenson discussed in this first call about the noise at the plant.

[Question 19 starts a Secondary T-Funnel about what was said in the first telephone call regarding noise at the plant]

20–22 [*Secondary T-Funnel questions and answers omitted*]

23. Q: After this first call to Mr. Stevenson, when was the next time you complained to someone about the plant?

[Question 23 seeks to identify the next event in the timeline definition]

24. A: Well a few weeks after I called Mr. Stevenson, I hadn't heard back from him so I decided I'd text Biderman, the guy who owned the plant, and tell him that he had to stop taking deliveries at night because they were making too much noise.

25. Q: Did you complain to anyone about the plant between your initial call with Mr. Stevenson and your text to Biderman?

[Question 25 checks for gaps before the next event identified]

26. A: No.

27. Q: Did you receive a response from Biderman?

28. Q: I got a text from that number that referred me to Josh Masse, the assistant manager of operations. The text gave me a phone number and said that I was welcome to call him.

29. Q: And did you speak with Mr. Masse?

30. A: Yes.

31. Between the time you first talked to Mr. Stevenson and the time you spoke with Mr. Masse did you make any complaints about the plant to anyone else?

[Question 31 checks for gaps before the next event identified]

32. A: No.

33. Q: When did you speak with Mr. Masse?

34. A: I called him right when I received the text, so maybe a few weeks after the call with Stevenson.

35. Q: And was it just you and Mr. Masse on that call?

[Questions 33 and 35 probe for Event Essentials]

36. A: Yes.

37. Q: All right, I'd like to go over this conversation with Mr. Masse just like we did with your first conversation with Mr. Stevenson. Why don't you tell me everything you discussed during that call?

[Question 37 starts a T-Funnel with an open question about what happened during the call with Masse]

38. A: Well, I told him that. . .

[T-Funnel questioning about what was discussed during this call omitted.]

6. ELICITING STORIES WHEN A DEPONENT CANNOT REMEMBER THE ORDER OF EVENTS

In the example above, the deponent recalls the order of complaints and can therefore provide a timeline. Of course, deponents sometimes are unable, or claim to be unable, to remember the chronological order in which events occurred. In such situations, you may abandon the timeline pattern and instead rely on T-Funnels to obtain complete information. Simply use T-Funnels to elicit testimony about events without regard to the order in which the events occurred.

The transcript below illustrates how you might rely on T-Funnel questioning of Ms. Terry about her complaints in the *Terry v. Biderman Construction Co,* case if she did not remember the order in which her complaints were made.

1. Q: Ms. Terry, you mentioned earlier that you complained about the plant and what was going on there. So I'd like to ask you about any complaints you made to anyone in any way related to the plant. If possible, I'd like to start at the beginning and go through each complaint

one by one. So could you tell me when was the first time you complained to someone about the plant?

2. A: I made lots of complaints to people. I don't really remember which one I made first or second or whatever.

3. Q: I realize it's hard to remember the order of all the complaints that you made but can you remember the first complaint you made?

4. A: I don't remember who I complained to first or when I did it. It was a long time ago and I just can't remember when things happened.

5. Q: Okay, I know it's hard to remember dates but do you remember approximately how long after the plant started operation that you made your first complaint?

6. A: It was about a month or so after they opened that plant.

7. Q: And can you remember to whom you made the first complaint?

8. A: I'm not sure. It may have been my city councilman, Mr. Stevenson, or the owner of the plant that I talked to first. I just can't recall.

9. Q: All right. Ms. Terry let's try this, maybe it will work easier for you. Just tell me all the things that you complained about at any time that were in any way related to the plant.

[Since the deponent is unable to provide a timeline, you turn to T-Funnel questions

beginning with the topic, "Things the deponent complained about"]

10. A: The biggest problem was the dust. It was everywhere. I couldn't keep it out of my house even when I kept all the windows closed.

11. Q: So the dust is one thing. Did you make any other complaints related in any way to the plant?

12. A: The noise. There were trucks parked on the streets at all hours of the night, there were deliveries at night and the trucks made all sorts of noise, especially the back-up beeping. And the owner of the plant was supposed to put up a screen to control the dust, but it was always falling apart and he wouldn't do anything about it for weeks at a time. I told Mr. Stevenson, my city councilman, about the dust and that I had to keep all my windows closed.

13. Q: Did you make any other complaints, other than about dust and noise, related in any way to the plant?

14. A: I had to go see the doctor several times because I was having breathing difficulties from all the dust in the air and in my house. And I complained to Mr. Stevenson that the city should never have let them build that plant.

15. Q: Did you ever complain about anything else?

16. A: No, that's about it.

17. Q: So the complaints you've told me about are the only significant ones that you had about the plant, is that right?

18. A: That's right.[2]

19. Q: Now Ms. Terry, I'd like you to tell me everyone that you complained to about the problems you had as a result of the operation of the plant.

[Having gotten a list of the deponent's complaints, you now begin a new T-Funnel, "People to whom the deponent complained"]

20. A: I complained to my city councilman, Mr. Stevenson, the owner of the plant, Mr. Biderman, Mr. Masse, who worked at the plant, my lawyer and the local newspaper.

21. Q: Did you complain to anyone else about the plant?

22. A: I don't think so.

23. Q: Did you complain to any of your neighbors?

24. A: Well, we talked about the problems all the time. But they were complaining to me as much as I was complaining to them.

---

[2] Note that in this example, examining counsel does not ask any closed questions at the bottom of the T-Funnel to suggest additional problems the deponent might have had. Whether or not to suggest additional damaging testimony by asking such questions at the bottom of the T-Funnel is a matter of judgment.

25. Q: Did you ever complain to a homeowners' association?

26. A: Yes, I did. I sent a letter to the homeowners' association asking them to do something about the noise and the dust.

27. Q: Did you complain about the plant to anyone else?

28. A: Well, I complained to my children about it all the time. Do you want to know about that?

29. Q: Sure. Maybe we can talk about that in a little while. Did you complain to anyone else?

30. A: No. That's it.

[T-Funnel #3—What deponent said to Stevenson]

31. Q: Now Ms. Terry, I'd like to find out what you and Mr. Stevenson, your city councilman, discussed regarding the problems you were having. So please tell me everything that you can recall that you said to Mr. Stevenson about the plant.

32. A: I know I told Mr. Stevenson about. . .

[Questioning continues to determine what the deponent said to Stevenson, and then goes on to explore her communications with other people]

Note that you may be able to obtain timelines for some topics but not others. For example, Ms. Terry may be unable to remember the order of her complaints about problems with the plant. However, Ms. Terry may have made three visits to the doctor for illnesses allegedly caused by the dust from the plant and, perhaps with the aid of the medical records obtained prior to the deposition, she may remember what happened during each visit. If so, you would be able to obtain a timeline of those visits.

CHAPTER 7

STRATEGIES FOR PINNING THE TALE ON THE DEPONENT

Chapters 5 and 6 describe the timeline and T-funnel questioning strategies that help you organize deponents' testimony into chronological stories while seeking to uncover and undermine harmful evidence and to uncover and bolster helpful evidence.

The strategies that this chapter describes are tools for expanding the scope and depth of timeline and T-funnel questioning. Not all of these tools will apply to every deposition you take. When you prepare to take depositions, you can decide which tools are likely to produce important evidence. But integrating questions that these tools generate into timeline and T-funnel questioning further your goals of pinning deponents to their stories and advancing the use of depositions for purposes of settlement and trial preparation.

1. FILL IN THE BLANKS

Thorough deposition questioning often depends on expanding stories by identifying and inquiring about events or topics that deponents have not mentioned. This section suggests two tools for using your own experience and knowledge as the basis of inquiries into these possibly "hidden" events or topics.

A. HISTORICAL RECONSTRUCTION

Historical reconstruction is a tool for using your experience about "how things typically happen" to generate questions about potential events and topics.[1] To use historical reconstruction ask yourself, "If the deponent's testimony is accurate, what else is likely to have happened?" Events, documents or other factors you identify in answer to this question are matters for potential inquiry. A deponent's testimony that harmful events did not unfold as such events typically do may undermine the deponent's credibility. Conversely, a deponent's testimony that helpful events unfolded as they usually do may strengthen your claim that testimony pertaining to the helpful events is credible.

For example, assume that you represent a terminated employee in an employment discrimination lawsuit. The manager of the defendant employer claims that your client was terminated for consistently coming to work under the influence of alcohol or drugs. Ask yourself, "If the manager's testimony is accurate, what else might be true?" Consistent happenings you might identify include:

- Complaints from other employees.
- Poor performance of work assignments.

---

[1] In addition to your everyday experience, you may base "fill in the blanks" questions on information you learn as cases progress, experts, colleagues and other sources.

- Evidence of possession of alcohol or drugs at the workplace.
- Warnings to the terminated employee.

Factors such as these become the subject matter of questions as you carry out timeline or T-funnel questioning.

B. "ESPECIALLY AND EXCEPT WHEN"

"Especially and except when" is a second tool for generating potential topics of inquiry. To use this tool, convert a deponent's factual assertion into a generalization. Then add "especially when" or "except when" to identify potential events or topics that tend to support or undermine the generalization. You can choose to pursue these events or topics during timeline or T-funnel questioning.

For an illustration of the "especially/except when" tool, return to the example in which the manager of a defendant employer testifies that your client was terminated for consistently coming to work under the influence of alcohol or drugs. Convert the testimony into a generalization: "Managers sometimes terminate employees for consistently coming to work under the influence of alcohol or drugs." By adding "especially when" to this generalization you may identify events and topics such as:

- The company has a policy against such behavior.
- The company tests employees randomly.

- The manager has previously warned an employee to seek treatment.
- Other employees have complained about the behavior to the manager.

And by adding "except when" to this generalization, you may identify events or topics such as:

- The manager has overlooked similar behavior by other employees.
- The employee has entered a company-authorized treatment program.
- The employee's work has been satisfactory.
- The employee's behavior has not been noted in performance reviews.

Depending on whether you seek to undermine harmful evidence or bolster the credibility of helpful evidence, the events or topics you identify can generate questions and answers tending to support or undermine the deponent's version of events.

2. PURSUE HEARSAY AND SPECULATION

Trial evidence rules require that lay witnesses testify from personal knowledge. But you can ask deponents about pertinent hearsay assertions made by or communicated to the deponent. When a hearsay statement advances your legal claims, you can also pursue foundational evidence that satisfies a hearsay exception or exemption. You can also ask deponents to testify about their beliefs or understandings about facts for which they have no first-hand or hearsay knowledge.

For example, assume that a deponent was not present for an important meeting. You might ask if the deponent knows who attended the meeting, what was discussed, what decisions were made, and the sources of the deponent's knowledge about these matters. You might also ask if the deponent communicated anything about the meeting to others, and to whom and in what form those communications were made. Similarly, you can ask a deponent to identify other individuals who the deponent believes might have knowledge about the meeting and ask the deponent for that belief. The answers will likely not be admissible at trial, but may be helpful in identifying additional sources of information.

3. ASK "WHY" AND "WHY NOT"

A party's motivation for engaging in conduct can be critical information. "Why" and "why not" questions can be effective tools for eliciting that information. For instance, assume you are deposing an employee of the defendant in an auto accident case. Your theory is that the defendant was negligent because he did not pay attention to the road prior to the accident. During your deposition of the employee, you learn that the defendant left a meeting early the day of the accident. You could lay foundation for a "why" question by asking the deponent, "Do you know why your boss left that meeting early?" If the deponent says "yes," you could then ask, "Why did defendant leave the meeting before it ended?" If the deponent responds, "The boss got a text indicating that a major project had failed a safety inspection," the answer to the "why" question supports your contention that the defendant was focused on the failed inspection and therefore drove carelessly.

"Why" questions can also help you avoid fruitless arguments. For example, perhaps your deposition questioning uncovers an adverse witness' prior inconsistent statement. If the case goes to trial, you may want to use the inconsistency to attack the deponent's credibility. But assume that at the deposition, you ask "why" the deponent made an inconsistent statement. If the deponent testifies to a reasonable explanation, you may avoid a fruitless and "pie in the face" impeachment attempt at trial.

4. ASK "HAVE YOU NOW TOLD ME EVERYTHING?"

Before concluding questioning with respect to an important event or other topic, consider asking a question such as, "Have you now told me everything you can recall (about the event or topic)?" Wrap-up questions such as this one may dissuade deponents from surprising you by expanding on their deposition testimony later in a case.

5. SEEK OUT OPINIONS AND THEIR BASES

Deponents may volunteer or you may intentionally seek opinions. For instance, a deponent may testify, "The supervisor constantly made rude and sexist comments" or you may ask whether in a deponent's opinion a defendant was driving too fast.

In either situation, pinning deponents down to their stories effectively includes pursuing the underlying bases for their opinions. If a deponent testifies that a building owner made a "good faith effort" to remedy code violations, follow up by asking the deponent to identify everything that the owner did to remedy the violations. Similarly, if in response to your question a deponent testifies that a car was not being driven dangerously fast for conditions, ask for all of the bases for that opinion.

Pinning witnesses down to opinions and their bases can be useful regardless of whether an opinion is harmful or helpful. If an opinion is harmful, follow-up questions can help to determine whether a deponent has sufficient personal knowledge to provide the opinion in the first place. In addition, eliciting the bases of harmful opinions can help you prepare to undermine them. And when opinions are helpful, obtaining their bases helps you to establish their admissibility and bolster their probative value.

6. PRESS FOR DETAILS

When deponents refer to conversations, meetings and other events, they may be content to refer to "the gist of what was said" or "the upshot of the meeting." But as an old saying goes, the "devil is in the details." To pin deponents down to their stories, push them to provide as much detail as they can. You can try to prompt the deponent's recollection of a meeting by using the timeline questioning technique to ask the deponent to describe the meeting by identifying the topics that were discussed in the meeting in the order they were discussed. You can also try to refresh the deponent's recollection by referring the deponent to other deponents' statements, documents or anything else that may promote recollection. And you might use the "historical reconstruction" and "especially/except when" tools to identify likely events and topics.

7. PARSE CLUMPED EVENTS

Effective pin-down questioning can include trying to parse "clumped events" into sub-happenings and then pursuing information about the sub-happenings individually. Understandably, a deponent may be unable to separate a clumped event into sub-happenings. In such circumstances your only choice other is to ask about the clumped event.

Example

A portion of a deposition of the supervisor in which you attempt to parse a clumped event into constituent sub-happenings prior to seeking details may go as follows:

Q: Did you talk with Ms. Gilbert about her sales reports?

A: Yes. Several times.

Q: What do you mean by several?

A: Four or five times, over a period of several weeks.

Q: Okay, can you remember the first time that you met with Ms. Gilbert about her sales reports?

A: They kind of all blend together. I'll try to answer as best as I can about individual meetings.

Q: Well let's start and see how it goes. That first meeting, do you remember when it took place?

A: I think it was early last May.

Q: And just with reference to that first meeting, please tell me as much as you can recall about what took place.

A: Well. . . .

8. SEEK EXAMPLES OF REPEATED BEHAVIOR

When deponents refer to behavior by testifying that it took place "repeatedly," "constantly," or use a similar term, ask them to identify specific instances when the behavior occurred. The strategy pins them to their stories while allowing you to evaluate the foundational basis and probative value of the testimony.

Example 1

A: Gibney constantly criticized me more harshly than the other salespeople anytime I failed to reach a sales quota.

Q: I want you to identify for me every time that Mr. Gibney criticized you more harshly than other salespeople for failing to reach a sales quota. Let's start by your describing for me the very first time that Mr. Gabney did that.

Example 2

A: Rosas repeatedly came to meetings unprepared to discuss proposals.

Q: You say "repeatedly." Please tell me the number of times that Rosas came to meetings unprepared to discuss a proposal.

A: I don't know for certain. Maybe five times.

Q: Please describe for me the first time that Rosas came to a meeting unprepared to discuss a proposal.

9. CLARIFY AMBIGUOUS REFERENCES AND GESTURES

Another pin down technique is to convert gestures and ambiguous references to verbal terms.

For example, if a deponent says that two people "were about as close as I am to you," ask the deponent on the record to estimate the distance between you and the deponent. Or you may ask, "Would you agree that the distance is about seven feet?"

And if a deponent testifies that in a physical altercation, the defendant struck the plaintiff "like this," and demonstrates how the plaintiff was struck, make sure that you elicit a verbal description of the demonstration for the record. Again, you might ask the deponent to describe what happened verbally. Or you might provide a description for the record and ask the deponent to confirm that your description is accurate.

CHAPTER 8

CEMENTING HELPFUL ANSWERS

Witnesses may be adverse yet nevertheless provide information that supports your legal claims. In such situations, cementing that information at deposition discourages adverse witnesses from post-deposition changes of stories by strengthening potential impeachment. This chapter reviews effective cementing strategies.

1. PIN DOWN HELPFUL ANSWERS

Cementing consists of pinning witnesses down to helpful deposition testimony by asking them to repeat it. Consider this brief example of testimony:

1. Q: Who attended the March 1 meeting?
2. A: Julie, Mario and Esteban were at the meeting.
3. Q: So Esteban was one of the attendees at the March 1 meeting?
4. A: Right.

Assuming that Esteban's presence at the March 1 meeting supports your legal claims, Nos. 3 and 4 cement the deponent's answer in No. 2. Asking the witness to repeat the answer greatly diminishes the chance that the deponent will later recant the answer and claim that "I misspoke" or "I was confused." And if the deponent at trial denies that Esteban was at the meeting, impeachment is likely to carry more weight because the witness testified twice to an inconsistent statement.

When helpful information is embedded in a longer portion of testimony, isolating the information with a separate question and answer exchange is a useful cementing strategy. If the deponent testifies inconsistently at trial your impeachment may have more impact. You can generally impeach based on the isolated statement alone without having to refer to the longer portion of testimony. Consider the next example.

You represent Seth Altman in an action against Four Star Mortgage Company based on a theory of fraudulent misrepresentation. Among other things, you seek to prove that Altman relied on a broker's misrepresentations. During your deposition of the Four Star broker who dealt with Seth, the following occurs:

1. Q: When you first called Mr. Altman on the 14th, what happened?

2. A: Not very much in this first call. We talked generally about mortgage interest rates and about how long the loan process would take. I said that Four Star had been in the mortgage business for a long time, that I had handled many loans for people who were in Mr. Altman's situation and that I would like to meet with him at his home to discuss a possible loan. Mr. Altman said he already had appointments to talk to some other brokers but that he would be willing to meet with me and we arranged to meet later in the week. I believe it was for the following Friday.

The deponent's testimony that (1) "Four Star had been in the mortgage business for a long time" and that (2) "I have handled many loans for people in Mr. Altman's situation" supports your legal claim that Altman relied on the broker's representations. But those statements were part of a longer answer. As a result you might cement the answers by isolating those statements:

3. Q: So when you first called Mr. Altman, you told him that Four Star had been in the mortgage business for a long time, correct?

4. A: Yes.

5. Q: And in this initial call to Mr. Altman, you also said you had handled many loans for people who were in Mr. Altman's situation, is that right?

6. A: Yes.

Note that questions Nos. 3 and 5 in the example above are leading. Cementing repeatedly with leading questions may send strong signals to the deponent that an answer helps your case. To prevent cementing from becoming more transparent than necessary, you may choose to cement with non-leading questions. For example, you might have phrased No. 3 as follows:

3. Q: What did you tell Mr. Altman about how long Four Star had been in the mortgage business?

2. CEMENT "SURROUNDING EVIDENCE"

To minimize the risk that cementing may lead a deponent to reconsider the accuracy of helpful information, you might camouflage the helpful answer by also cementing surroundings information that you don't really care about. Like a magician, you hope the verbal "sleight of hand" deflects attention from your real goal. For example, in the above example you might ask, "And you also talked to Mr. Altman about the usual length of the loan process?"

3. DELAY CEMENTING

You need not always cement as soon as a deponent provides a helpful answer. Immediate cementing may lead a deponent to wiggle away from a helpful answer. If you delay cementing, a deponent and opposing counsel may think that you are doing nothing more than briefly recapping a portion of the deponent's story.

4. USE THE DEPONENT'S OWN WORDS

You can further reduce a deponent's suspicions by cementing in a deponent's own words. This practice avoids any intimation that you are trying to put words into a deponent's mouth.

5. OFFER A NEUTRAL EXPLANATION FOR CEMENTING

Another strategy for obscuring the helpfulness of cemented testimony is to offer a neutral reason for repeating testimony. Common reasons you can offer include:

- Clarifying chronology. For example: "So that we're clear on time, the meeting was held on March 1?"
- Pretending your notes are unclear. For example: "Just to make sure my notes are accurate, during that first call, you told Mr. Altman that you had experience handling loans for people in his situation, correct?"
- Providing a summary. For example:
    - Q: So by way of summary, in this first call with Mr. Altman, you discussed mortgage rates, correct?
    - A: Yes.
    - Q: And you discussed the length of the loan process in that first call, correct?
    - A: Correct.
    - Q: And you explained how long Four Star had been in the mortgage business during that first call, correct?
    - A: Yes.

6. ACCREDIT HELPFUL INFORMATION

Bolstering the credibility of helpful deposition testimony further diminishes the potential for a later change in a story. For example, you may accredit a helpful answer with testimony that a deponent has a good reason to recall the information: "Are people seeking loans generally reassured when you tell them you've been in the mortgage business for a long time?"

7. OBTAIN AN EVIDENTIARY FOUNDATION

Evidence rules may prevent you from offering helpful deposition testimony at trial. For example, a deponent may testify about information in a business record, but "former testimony" evidence rules may allow the adversary to make for the first time or renew a deposition hearsay objection if you seek to offer the record into evidence at trial. Similarly, an adversary may be able to make for the first time or renew a deposition "lack of foundation" or "lack of personal knowledge" objection when you seek to offer opinion testimony into evidence at trial. To overcome potential trial objections such as these, seek to satisfy evidentiary requirements during depositions. For example you might elicit foundational evidence that makes a business record or an "excited utterance" admissible and elicit foundational evidence that supports the admissibility of deponents' opinions.

8. CEMENT "THAT'S ALL"

Answers such as "that's all" or "I don't remember anything else" can be helpful to cement because they discourage deponents from adding post-deposition information. You can cement these responses to the same extent as any other helpful answer. For example, assume that in a wrongful termination case a deponent testifies, "Orin was terminated because of excessive tardiness and insubordination." You may cement follows:

1. Q: Did you have any other reasons for the termination?

2. A: No, just the two I mentioned.

3. Q: So that I'm clear, the two reasons for terminating Orin were excessive tardiness and insubordination?

4. A: Correct.

5. Q: And these are the only reasons that you fired Orin, right?

6. A: Yes.

9. "ASKED AND ANSWERED" OBJECTIONS

When you cement helpful evidence, opposing counsel may object on the ground of "Asked and Answered." The objection is improper so long as cementing does not amount to witness harassment. Therefore, treat such an objection as you would any other improper objection to form: ignore the objection and ask the deponent to answer your question.

10. COMMUNICATE ARGUMENTS

Closely akin to the strategy of cementing helpful evidence is the strategy of using depositions as opportunities to communicate your arguments to adversaries. This strategy can be particularly helpful when a deponent is the adverse party.

By communicating directly with the adverse party, you limit the ability of the adversary's lawyer to misrepresent or water down your legal position when communicating your position to your adversary. Instead, you have a chance to improve the chance for settlement by (1) impressing the adversary with the reasonableness and cogency of your legal claims; and (2) demonstrating to the adversary that the cross-examination style of questioning that communicating arguments involves is unpleasant and not an experience the adversary wants to repeat at trial.

For example, assume you represent families who bought affordable housing in a new sub-division in an action against the developer for the serious illnesses they experienced because of the developer's concealing that the houses were built on land polluted with carcinogenic chromium that affected the land's water supply. The deponent, the president of the development company who is your adversary, denies that the company knew about the pollution. You might communicate an argument that the company was aware of the pollution with leading questions such as:

> Q: Your position is that the company was unaware that the land was polluted by carcinogenic chromium?
>
> Q: But you knew that an abandoned metallurgy plant had occupied much of the parcel for decades, correct?

Q: You knew at the time of the purchase of the parcel that another developer had made and then withdrawn an offer to buy the land, correct?

Q: And the construction crews who worked on the project developed serious and unusual illnesses, right?

Q: And your company paid crew members' medical costs in return for their agreement not to report their illnesses to the County Health Department?

Q: . . . .

You do not ask questions such as these in order to uncover new information. Instead, you communicate an argument by marshalling information that you are already aware of. The strategy may enhance your settlement position by impressing an adversary with the strength of an argument you will make if the case goes to trial while reminding the adversary that cross examination will not be a pleasant experience.

CHAPTER 9

UNDERMINING HARMFUL TESTIMONY

Depositions are an opportunity not only to pin adverse witnesses to their stories but also to seek to undermine the credibility of harmful evidence. This chapter first examines common factors to weigh when deciding whether to undermine harmful statements, and then provides several questioning strategies you can employ if you decide to try to do so.

1. SHOULD YOU PROBE CREDIBILITY?

Compared to trials, depositions generally afford you with a greater opportunity to decide whether you want to probe adverse deponents' credibility. This section identifies common circumstances that can help you to decide whether to devote deposition time to seeking to undermine the credibility of harmful evidence.

One factor is your assessment of the likelihood that a deponent will be unavailable to testify at trial. If a deponent is unavailable to testify at trial, your adversary will probably be able to offer the deponent's deposition testimony into evidence. If so, the deposition may be your best and perhaps only chance to get into the record evidence that undermines the credibility of the deponent's story.

A second factor to consider when deciding whether to seek to undermine harmful evidence is whether you can produce extrinsic evidence that undermines the credibility of (i.e., rebuts) an adverse witness' deposition testimony. If you have evidence in the form of documents or witnesses that you can refer to during settlement discussions or offer into evidence at trial that undermines the credibility of harmful evidence, you may choose not to probe a deponent's credibility at a deposition.

A third factor is an adversary's knowledge that you can produce extrinsic evidence that undermines the credibility of an adverse deponent's testimony. Assume that your assessment is that an adversary is not aware that you can produce extrinsic evidence that undermines the credibility of harmful testimony. In this circumstance, you may choose not to seek to undermine harmful evidence at a deposition. You may thereby surprise an adversary with your evidence during settlement discussions or at trial, while minimizing the adversary's ability to gather evidence that might rebut your extrinsic evidence.

A fourth factor is the likelihood that a case will settle prior to trial. If settlement is almost certainly in the offing, you may advance your settlement position by seeking to undermine the credibility of harmful deposition testimony at the deposition.

Finally, recall that you may take a deposition in the hope that an adversary will recognize that settlement is a much less stressful option than going to trial. You can probably advance this goal by engaging in aggressive and thorough (yet civil) questioning that seeks to undermine the credibility of harmful evidence.

2. STRATEGIES FOR CHALLENGING DEPONENTS' CREDIBILITY

This section examines four questioning strategies you can employ in an attempt to undermine harmful testimony:

- Challenge the accuracy of the testimony
- Undermine the inference to be drawn from the testimony
- Aggrandize the lie
- Probe opinions, conclusions and behavior over time

Each of these approaches can help you cast doubt on the accuracy or the probative value of harmful evidence.

A. CHALLENGE THE ACCURACY

One way to potentially undermine harmful testimony is to elicit evidence suggesting that the testimony is inaccurate. You may choose to probe one or more of the following factors to search for evidence that a harmful statement is untrue.

- **Bias or Motive**

Bias and motive are familiar factors suggesting that a deponent's emotional or financial stake in a dispute's outcome inclines the deponent to tell a story that favors your adversary. Evidence suggesting a bias or motive is a basis on which you can argue that a deponent is either consciously lying or subconsciously slanting evidence in favor of an adversary.

At the same time, witnesses are commonly subject to claims of bias based on personal or professional relationships. For example, a deponent may be employed by or socially acquainted with an adverse party. Much the same is likely to be true of the witnesses who provide information helpful to your clients.

As a result, general claims of bias are easy to make and often of little value. However, you might be able to undermine the credibility of harmful testimony if you can develop evidence of a deponent's "particularized bias or motive" that goes beyond mere party association. Three ways of probing for particularized bias include:

- Special gain or loss: Does a deponent stand to gain financial or social benefits by testifying for your adversary? For example, are the deponent and your adversary in related industries such that testimony in your adversary's interest is also in the deponent's interest?

- Closeness of relationship with the adversary: Does the deponent have a particularly strong bond with your adversary? For example, do the deponent and your adversary have a long social or professional relationship?

- Hostility toward your client: Does the deponent have reason to dislike your client or anyone else on your side of the case?

- **Reason for Recall**

You might be able to undermine the credibility of harmful evidence if you uncover information casting doubt on a deponent's ability to recall the harmful evidence. Examples:

- A harmful event is routine. For example, a grocery store clerk describes items that a customer purchased or a waiter in a busy restaurant describes a conversation between four diners. How many similar events does the deponent participate in during the average day? How is the deponent able to recall such a fungible event? If the deponent cannot provide a reason why the routine event was memorable, you can argue there is no reason to recall the harmful testimony and thus the testimony should not be believed.
- A deponent describes a harmful event that took place in the somewhat distant past. For example, a broker testifies about a negotiation that took place two years ago. Why does the deponent remember the details of the negotiation given how long ago it took place? Does the deponent also recall other things that were taking place at the same time? If not, you can argue that there is no reason for the deponent to recall the harmful testimony and thus it should not be believed.

Sometimes when you probe for evidence that an event is routine or ancient, a deponent may provide a credible reason for why they remember. Such an explanation may be harmful, but it is better to find out at the deposition than at a less opportune time later in the case! You can try to undermine that harmful explanation using the techniques in this chapter, and if ultimately you find deponent's harmful story credible, at a minimum, you may reassess your client's settlement posture.

- **Details, Details**

You might be able to undermine the credibility of harmful evidence by demonstrating that a deponent is unable to describe details of events that we would reasonably expect a person to be able to provide if a story were accurate. For example, a deponent provides damaging testimony about what she observed your client doing while she was watching a performance of *Hamlet*, but she can't recall what an actor said after the words, "To be or . . ."

By the same token, a deponent may provide so many insignificant details that a story lacks credulity for that reason. For example, one of the authors was involved in a case in which one of the parties testified about a lengthy negotiation that had taken place about 15 years earlier. The party lost credibility by claiming to recall not only a plethora of mundane details but also the order in which topics were addressed during the negotiation.

- **Absence of Corroborative Evidence**

Another way to challenge the accuracy of harmful testimony is to demonstrate that it is not corroborated by documents or other witnesses.

Consequently, when faced with harmful testimony, you may routinely ask questions such as:

- "Are you aware of any documents that pertain to what you discussed at the meeting?"
- "Do you know of any documents that can corroborate what you've told me?"
- "Are you aware of any witnesses who can confirm what you've told me?"
- "Are you aware of any witnesses who you believe would disagree with what you've told me?"

Inquiries such as these can help you determine if the harmful answer can be corroborated and may also identify additional areas of inquiry or potential additional witnesses and documents.

- **Inability to Perceive**

Another strategy for seeking to challenge harmful testimony is to elicit evidence that the deponent lacked an adequate ability to perceive. For example, if a deponent was far away from the harmful event, or if there were obstacles between the deponent and the event the deponent claims to have observed, you can argue that the harmful testimony should not be believed because the deponent was not in a position to perceive it accurately.

You can search for both external obstacles (i.e., distance, physical obstructions, lighting, weather, and noise) and internal obstacles to perception (i.e., stress, emotional state, hearing impairments, poor eyesight, drug use or intoxication).

- **Inconsistent Statements**

Evidence that a deponent has given inconsistent accounts of a harmful event is a common factor that tends to undermine the credibility of a deponent's story.

If you are aware at the time of a deposition that a deponent has given inconsistent accounts of an event, a useful strategy is to ask the deponent for an explanation of the inconsistency. You hope, of course, that the deponent cannot explain an inconsistency in a way that makes sense. But if a deponent can provide a reasonable explanation, you prefer to find out at the deposition rather than later. At least you then have an opportunity to gather additional information demonstrating that the explanation is itself not credible.

You may be aware of a statement made by another witness, or that is in a document, that contradicts a deponent's account of a harmful event. You might reveal the inconsistency to the deponent and perhaps undermine the deponent's version of the event by asking the deponent to explain why the other witness or the document differs from the deponent's account.

More likely, depositions provide you with an opportunity to learn about sources of possible inconsistent statements. For example:

- Did a deponent make a written record of an event? If so, ask for a copy and check to see whether the previous record is inconsistent with the deponent's testimony.

- Did the deponent speak to other people about an event? If so, obtain contact information for the people to whom the deponent spoke and later ask for the account that the deponent gave them.
- Does the deponent know of other people who might have knowledge of the same harmful event? If so, ask about their identities and follow up to find out if their accounts of the event differ from the deponent's.

- **Inconsistent Behavior**

Another strategy for seeking to undermine harmful evidence is to search for information suggesting that a deponent's story lacks credibility because the story is inconsistent with the deponent's prior or subsequent actions. If the deponent makes a harmful statement but is unable to provide a coherent story of what happened before or after that harmful event consistent with what you would expect to have happened, you can argue that the harmful statement is not accurate. Examples:

- A deponent testifies he observed a startling incident that is harmful to your client. What did the deponent do after the event had concluded? Did the deponent make a record of what took place? If so, what did the deponent do with the record? Did the deponent report what happened to anyone? If the deponent cannot provide this type of testimony, you have elicited evidence you can use to argue the harmful statement should not be believed.

- A deponent testifies she participated in an important meeting which undercuts your theory of the case. Did the deponent prepare for the meeting? What did the deponent do to prepare? Did the deponent talk to anyone about what took place at the meeting? Did the deponent make a record of what took place at the meeting? Again, if the deponent cannot provide this type of testimony, you have elicited testimony you can use to argue the deponent did not actually participate in the meeting.

Once you have established that the deponent has engaged in arguably inconsistent behavior, you may want to ask "why" and "why not" questions to evaluate whether the deponent has a plausible explanation for the behavior.

- **Implausible Statements**

Implausible statements are those that conflict with common everyday experience. For instance, it is implausible for an athlete who claims to have won an Olympic gold medal to be unable to identify the city or date of the triumph. And it is implausible for a person to be unjustly fired from a job that the person loved and yet claim, "I wasn't in the least upset by the firing."

If a deponent's account of a harmful event strikes you as implausible, as with an inconsistent statement a useful strategy is to find out whether the deponent has an explanation that vitiates the seeming implausibility. Ask "why" and "why not" questions. "Why can't you remember where the Olympics were held?" "Why weren't you upset about being fired?" It may turn out the deponent has a plausible explanation. For example, it may be that the fired employee wasn't upset because "Just before I was fired, I had found out that I won the state lottery." But if a deponent can reasonably explain away a seeming implausibility you want to find out about it at deposition rather than later in the case.

Even if a deponent's account of a harmful event is plausible "on its face," you may seek to elicit further evidence suggesting its implausibility. You may use case-specific information you have learned from other sources as the basis of your inquiries. The classic courtroom comedy film *My Cousin Vinny* (1992) has a great example of this strategy. A prosecution witness has tied two defendants to the murder of a store clerk. His seemingly-plausible story is that he saw the defendants enter and leave the store, and that they were in the store for only five minutes, the time it took him to prepare his breakfast. Defense lawyer Vinny demonstrates the implausibility of the five-minute estimate by eliciting evidence that the witness had grits for breakfast, and then confronting the witness with his recently-acquired knowledge that grits have to cook for twenty minutes before they are ready to eat.

Similarly, assume that you represent a plaintiff in a wrongful termination case in which the employer claims that the plaintiff was justly fired for insubordination. The deponent is a supervisor who testifies to the plaintiff's insubordinate acts. Based on information you have gathered, you might ask the deponent about actions of other employees who were insubordinate but not terminated. The answers may suggest that the stated reason for your client's termination is implausible.

Everyday experience rather than case-specific information you have gathered may also serve as the basis of questions seeking to establish that a deponent's story is implausible. Assume that a deponent was a driver waiting to turn left at an intersection. The deponent describes an incident that took place on a sidewalk near the intersection. Everyday experience may serve as the basis of questions suggesting that the deponent's story is implausible as most people in the deponent's position would have been too focused on the traffic and streetlights to observe the incident on the sidewalk closely.

B. ATTACK THE INFERENCE

A second strategy for undermining the credibility of a harmful event is to undercut the inference your adversary is likely to want to draw from the event. This approach is potentially available whenever a harmful event constitutes circumstantial evidence. To use this strategy, identify your adversary's likely desired inference and then identify circumstances tending to make the desired inference less likely to be true.

The "except when" technique is an effective method of identifying evidence tending to undercut an adversary's desired inference. You think, "The adversary's inference may be accurate, except when. . ." As you complete this sentence, the "except whens" you identify constitute potential evidence tending to undercut your adversary's desired inference.

For example, assume that you represent the plaintiff in a wrongful termination case. You contend that your client was terminated because of her gender; the defendant contends that the termination was for poor work performance. At deposition, the deponent is your client's former supervisor who testifies that one reason for your client's termination was her failure to meet her sales quota in the six month period immediately prior to her termination. You want to undermine your adversary's inference that the failure to meet the sales quota led to termination for poor work performance.

To identify topics you might ask about to try to undercut your adversary's inference, think:

An employee is likely to be terminated for failing to meet a sales quota, except when:

- Other employees failed to meet the quota but were not terminated.
- The employee misses the quota by a small margin.
- The employee has generally met sales quotas.

- Missing the sales quota was not mentioned in the employee's evaluation.
- The person who made the ultimate decision to terminate the employee did not know of the failure to meet the quota.

You would then inquire about these potential exceptions. Testimony that any of these exceptions exist would tend to undercut the inference your adversary seeks to draw from the harmful evidence.

C. AGGRANDIZE THE LIE

A third strategy for dealing with harmful testimony is to aggrandize the lie. This approach may make sense when you can convincingly contradict the deponent's harmful answer through a more credible witness or document. In taking this approach, you operate on the assumption that if a deponent is willing to embellish an answer that you can later clearly show is false, you can argue that the deponent has consciously lied, rather than made an innocent mistake, and thus should not be believed. And, as we all recognize, factfinders and settlement conference judges tend to view much more harshly witnesses they perceive to be lying rather than merely mistaken.

To aggrandize a lie, encourage a deponent to expand or elaborate on a harmful answer. For instance, you might ask a deponent to repeat a harmful statement and then encourage deponent to provide you with other details surrounding the harmful observation, or the reasons why they recall the harmful answer. These aggrandizing questions make it difficult for a deponent to later claim, "I made an innocent misstatement at deposition."

D. UNDERMINE OPINIONS, CONCLUSIONS, AND BEHAVIOR OVER TIME

When a deponent's harmful testimony consists of a conclusion or an opinion rather than a concrete perception or event, you can attempt to undermine it with testimony that the deponent has no (or an insufficient) basis for the opinion or conclusion. For example, if a deponent testifies that your client was rude to customers, you can ask the deponent to provide any concrete observations that support the opinion that your client was rude:

- "Tell me all the reasons you concluded my client was rude to customers."
- "What did you observe that led you to believe my client was being rude?"

If your questioning shows a lack of concrete observations supporting the harmful opinion or conclusion, you can argue the harmful testimony is not credible because there is no basis to support it.

Similarly, sometimes a deponent's harmful testimony is not about what took place on a single occasion, but instead constitutes a generalization about behavior over time. For example, in a wrongful termination case, a supervisor of the defendant company might assert that the plaintiff was "always late for work" or "almost never finished an assignment on time."

To try to undermine harmful testimony regarding conditions or behavior over time, you might proceed as follows:

- **Ask for specific instances.** Begin by asking deponents for specific instances of the behavior or condition. Example: "Mr. Supervisor, please give me a specific instance in which the plaintiff failed to finish his work assignment on time." Again, if a deponent has few or no concrete instances to support a harmful statement concerning a behavior or condition over time, you may later argue that the harmful statement is not credible because it lacks sufficient support.

- **Exhaust the deponent's memory.** Continue pressing deponents for specific instances until you have exhausted a deponent's recall. Example: "Mr. Supervisor, can you recall any other instances in which the plaintiff failed to finish his work assignment on time?"

- **Undermine the specific instances.** Once a deponent has testified to all the specific instances, you may decide to try to undermine them using any of the strategies described earlier in this Chapter. For example, to challenge accuracy you might ask questions such as: "Supervisor, what did you do after my client failed to turn in the August sales report on time?" *[probing for inconsistent behavior]* or "How is it that you can now remember that my client failed to complete the August sales report on time?" *[probing for inability to recall]*.

A Checklist for Undermining Harmful Answers

Below you will find a Checklist that summarizes the various approaches you might pursue to undermine a harmful answer. You can take this Checklist (or a customized version of it) with you to depositions to help you quickly come up with topics and questions for undermining harmful testimony. Additionally, you can use the Checklist during deposition preparation when you intend to question a deponent about harmful evidence of which you are already aware.

Of course this Checklist cannot be used like a cookie cutter to respond to all harmful testimony. You have to use your judgment to decide when to try to undermine harmful testimony and which strategies to use.

Checklist for Undermining Harmful Evidence

Challenge the Accuracy of the Evidence

- Bias or Motive
- Reason for Recall
- Details, Details
- Absence of Corroborative Evidence
- Inability to Perceive
- Inconsistent Statements
- Inconsistent Behavior

- Implausible Statements

Attack the Inference

- What inference would the other side like to draw?
- Are there circumstances that might make the other side's inference unlikely to be true?

Aggrandize the Lie

- Have the deponent repeat and expand on the harmful evidence.

Opinions, Conclusions and Behavior over Time

- Probe for the basis (if any) of the statement
- Undermine any discrete harmful observations the deponent provides

CHAPTER 10

RESPONDING TO EVASIVE, FORGETFUL OR UNCERTAIN DEPONENTS

When deponents use weasel words, are evasive or forgetful, you may need to do a little extra work to create clear answers that pin deponents to their stories. The strategies in the chapter will help you identify and respond to a variety of unsatisfactory types of answers.

1. EVASIVE DEPONENTS

This section provides suggestions for responding to evasive answers.

A. NON-RESPONSIVE ANSWERS

Non-responsive answers evade questions by providing a response to a question that is different from the one asked. Such responses can appear to provide a desired answer without actually doing so. For example:

Q: The bear went over the mountain, right?

A: Where else would it have gone?

The answer is evasive because the deponent does not explicitly answer the question. The simplest strategy for obtaining a responsive answer is to re-ask the question:

Q: The bear went over the mountain, right?

A: Where else would it have gone?

Q: So the bear did go over the mountain, correct?

A: Yes.

When you re-ask a question you may want to first indicate that you heard the answer:

Example 1

1. Q: Were you concerned about having the computers networked when they were installed?

2. A: I was concerned about getting them installed before our January push.

3. Q: I understand that you were concerned about getting the computers installed before the January push. But first I'd like to know whether you were concerned about having the computers networked when they were installed?

Example 2

1. Q: Did you review Exhibit 27, the third draft of the Environmental Impact Report, with your supervisor?

2. A: That's what I typically do.

3. Q: Okay, so you typically review these reports with your supervisor. But my question is, did you review Exhibit 27 with your supervisor?

B. SUMMARY CONCLUSIONS

Summary conclusions are another form of evasiveness. A deponent may suggest that there's nothing more to say about a topic with a summary statement such as:

- That was the **substance** of the discussion.
- Those are the **main things** we talked about.
- That was **about it**.

Responses such as this are hints that a deponent may be able to provide further information. An effective strategy for seeking further information is to refer to the "hint" and ask a follow-up question. For example:

1. Q: What did you discuss at the meeting early in June?

2: A: We talked about the acceptability of the specifications, the price per unit and the delivery date.

3: Q: Did you discuss anything else at this meeting?

4. A: Those were the main things we discussed.

5. Q: I understand you have told me the main things but I would like to know everything that was discussed at the meeting, regardless of how significant the topic was. In addition to the main things you mentioned, what else did you discuss?

6. A: I remember we talked very briefly about what to do if delivery was late.

7. Q: So you discussed acceptability of the specifications, the price per unit, the delivery date, and what to do if delivery was late. Did you discuss anything else at this meeting?

8. A: No.

9. Q: Did you discuss subcontracting some of your work?

10. A: No.

11. Q: How about changing specifications as the job developed. Was that discussed?

12. A: Now that you mention it, that was discussed.

Here, you pursue the hint (No. 5), and use a short T-funnel sequence to pursue possible additional topics (Nos. 7–12).

C. "WHAT DO YOU MEAN BY. . ." ANSWERS

Deponents may try to evade questions by claiming not to understand everyday words. For example:

1. Q: After you were hired as an appraiser, did anyone provide you with any training to help you do your job?

2. A: What do you mean by training?

One strategy for overcoming this form of evasion is to ask for and adopt a deponent's understanding of a term. For instance, in the above example, you might respond as follows:

3. Q: Ms. Mendez, what do you understand the word to mean?

4. A: I think it means giving me instructions or materials on how to do my job.

5. Q: All right. When I use the word training I mean exactly what you understand the term to mean. So let me ask you again, after you were hired as an appraiser did the company give you any training to help you do your job?

This approach hopefully discourages the deponent from engaging in this tactic. Of course, if the deponent's definition of a term is particularly narrow or highly idiosyncratic, you may have to follow up with additional questions to obtain complete information. For example:

6. Q: Ms. Mendez, do you have an understanding of what the word "training" means?

7. A: Yes, but I don't know what you mean when you say training.

8. Q: What do you understand the word to mean?

9. A: I think it means giving me formal classroom instruction to help me learn how to do my job.

10. Q: Let's use your definition for the moment. After you were hired as an appraiser did anyone

give you any training to help you learn how to do your job?

11. A: No.

12. Q: OK. For now let's assume that training means anything that anyone did to help you learn your job. Did you receive any of this type of training?

13. A: Well, I talked to a couple of my supervisors about. . .

D. OVERLY LITERAL OR HYPER-TECHNICAL DEPONENTS

Another form of evasion consists of a highly technical or overly literal interpretation of a question. For example, assume that a deponent once saw a report in which a defendant wrote that the plaintiff was lazy. When asked at deposition, "Did the defendant ever say the plaintiff was lazy?" the deponent responds either, "No" or "I don't know." A hyper-technical deponent may interpret the word "say" in your question to mean "say orally," thereby justifying the "No" or "I don't know" response.

When you suspect that a deponent might be using this kind of interpretive ploy to withhold information, you may respond with one (or more) of the following questioning techniques.

1. Avoid Making Your Questions Too Narrow

One way to keep deponents from engaging in this kind of evasion is to avoid using words in your questions that are too narrow. For example, if you ask, "Tell me everyone who attended the January 6, 2021 meeting", a deponent may interpret your question to ask only for those persons who attended the meeting in person, and not those who participated by phone or Zoom. You can avoid this problem by broadening the scope of your question: "Tell me everyone who attended the January 6, 2021 meeting regardless of whether it was in person, by phone or remotely."

2. Use a Series of Questions Containing Synonyms

Another strategy is to ask a series of questions that identify synonyms for a particular topic. For example:

1. Q: Ms. Lester, did Mr. Freeman ever say anything indicating that he disliked working with my client?

2. A: No.

3. Q: Did Mr. Freeman ever say that he personally disliked my client?

4. Q: Did Mr. Freeman ever say that he did not want to be part of a team with my client?

5. Q: So is it accurate to say that you are not aware of anything that Mr. Freeman spoke negatively about my client?

Use of synonyms for "disliked working with" may overcome a deponent's reliance on a hyper-technical meaning of common words.

3. Ask for Information from All Sources

Hyper-technical deponents may withhold information by distinguishing between information they have perceived directly and information based on hearsay. For example, you ask a deponent, "Did A ever strike B?", and the deponent answers "No" because the deponent didn't personally see it, even though the deponent had been told by others that A struck B.

Similarly, hyper-technical deponents may withhold information by making a distinction between what people have said and what they have written or done. For instance, you ask a deponent, "Did Hsu ever say he disliked my client?" The deponent answers "No," even though the deponent saw Hsu's email messages that were critical of the client, or saw Hsu make a disgusted gesture when a colleague mentioned your client. You may respond to these forms of withholding with a strategy called "expand the sources."

For instance, ask questions such as, "Are you aware of any information from any source whatsoever that might indicate that Hsu disliked my client?" A variation of this technique is to refer separately to what a deponent may have seen and heard: "Have you ever read anything in which Hsu indicated dislike for my client? Have you ever heard anything in which Hsu indicated dislike for my client?"

2. RESPONDING TO "I CAN'T REMEMBER," "I'M NOT SURE" AND "I DON'T KNOW"

A deponent may testify to a partial or complete failure of memory. For example, a deponent may not know of a meeting, may know of a meeting but not recall what took place, or may remember only a portion of the meeting. Similarly, a deponent may express uncertainty: "I think that Carl pushed for an alternative algorithm at that meeting but I'm not sure."

First, recognize that lack of knowledge, inability to recall and uncertainty may constitute helpful evidence that you want to cement. (See Ch.8.) One reason is that the deponent's weak memory means that an adversary cannot rely on the deponent to contradict evidence you may offer. And if the deponent does at a later time provide details that the deponent could not provide at the deposition, the deposition testimony is an inconsistent statement that provides you with an opportunity to impeach.

But "I don't know" and "I don't recall" types of responses may frustrate your efforts to obtain helpful information that you think a deponent may be able to provide. In these circumstances, you may use one or more of the following strategies.

- **Refresh Recollection**

A familiar strategy is to ask a witness to review a writing, a video or audio recording, a portion of a different deposition, or anything that communicates information about the topic you want to pursue. After a deponent has had a chance to review the material, ask if the deponent is now able to recall additional information. You may preface the questions with an empathic remark along these lines:

> "I understand that you may not be able to remember everything that was discussed at the August 15th meeting. But please review "X" and tell me as much as you can remember."

- **Bracket to Obtain a Best Estimate**

When questions seek numbers or dates, deponents may respond with "I don't know" or "I don't recall" when what they mean is, "I can't be precise." In such circumstances, the "bracketing" strategy may enable you to gain additional information. Bracketing tends to encourage deponents who are unwilling or unable to provide exact numbers to offer estimates of the upper and lower limits of a range within which their answers lie. Consider this example:

Q: On what date did you first meet Ms. Kekorian?

A: I don't know.

Q: Might it have been as early as April of last year?

A: I don't think so.

Q: Could it have been during May?

A: That's possible.

Q: Could it have been as late as August?

A: No, I'm sure it was before that.

Q: So your first meeting with Ms. Kekorian probably took place sometime between May and July of last year?

A: I'd say that's right.

Bracketing can also help you obtain estimates of distance. For example, you ask a deponent to state "the distance between the two cars after the collision." The deponent replies, "I'm really not sure." You may continue as follows:

Q: Would you say the distance was at least 10 feet?

A: I'm sorry, I'm just not sure.

Q: Would you say it was at least 5 feet, that's about the distance between you and me?

A: Yes, I'd have to say they were at least that far apart.

Q: All right. Could they have been more than 20 feet apart, that's probably a few feet longer than the length of this room?

A: No, they weren't that far apart.

Q: So after the accident the cars were somewhere between 5 and 20 feet apart, is that correct?

A: Yes, I'd agree with that.

- **Use Leading Questions**

You may also turn to closed or leading questions to seek information that deponents can't provide on their own. Leading questions are permissible when you depose adverse witnesses and may be an effective strategy to uncover information that witnesses can't otherwise provide.

- **Probe for Alternative Sources**

When despite your best efforts deponents do not produce additional information, you may try to use them as leads to alternative sources of information. One strategy is to ask deponents how they might go about finding the information. For example, you might proceed as follows:

Q: Approximately when did that meeting take place?

A: I really couldn't tell you, it was so long ago.

Q: If you wanted to find out when the meeting took place, what could you do to get that information.

A: I could ask my assistant Jerry Prager.

Q: Great, I'll follow up with Mr. Prager. Is there anyone else you could talk to in order to find out when the meeting took place?

A: No.

Q: Anything else you might do to check the date of the meeting?

A. Not that I can think of.

Q: Are there any documents you could review to refresh your recollection of when that meeting took place?

A: I could check my office calendar.

Q: Any other documents you could review to refresh your recollection?

A: No.

CHAPTER 11
MANAGING EXHIBITS

Exhibit-centered questioning is a routine and often critical feature of deposition-taking. For example, you may ask a deponent to:

- Comment on the content of an email message or a photograph;
- Lay the foundation establishing that a written or electronic document is a business record;
- Refresh recollection by looking at a purchase order or the minutes of a Board meeting;
- Mark up a diagram that traces the movement of a car prior to a collision;
- Identify the voices on a recording; or
- Explain the preparation of a computer animation.

Once they become the subject of deposition questioning, written and electronic records such as these become exhibits. And your most important questioning tasks typically involve establishing exhibits' authenticity and creating a record that clearly identifies the exhibits to which your questions refer. This chapter focuses on these tasks.

1. MAINTAIN A CLEAR RECORD

A "clear record" is one that allows a person who was not present at a deposition to identify the exhibits to which questions and answers refer. A common process for maintaining a clear record includes the following steps.

- **Describe Identifying Characteristics**

Assume you question a deponent about an exhibit by saying something along the lines of, "Take a look at this. Have you ever seen it before?" A person reading, listening to or watching the deposition and having access to the exhibits may have no idea which exhibit you are talking about. To maintain a clear record, when you question a deponent about an exhibit, first describe identifying characteristics of the document and then reference it by an exhibit number or letter. A description is typically a brief unique characteristic that distinguishes one exhibit from all other exhibits. For example:

- "I am holding a three-page document that has been Bates numbered ABC00024–ABC000026." (A "Bates number" is a combination of letters and numbers that is applied, either physically or electronically, to every document produced in the litigation so that each document has a unique Bates number. The letters typically signify who produced the document.)
- "I am holding a one-page document that identifies the sender as Santa Claus and the recipient as Tooth Fairy."
    - Or, if there are documents on different dates from the same sender to the same recipient: "I am holding a one-page document dated Dec. 25 that identifies the

sender as Santa Claus and the recipient as Tooth Fairy."

- Or, if there are other emails from the same sender to the same recipient with the same date: "I am holding a one-page document dated Dec. 25 that identifies the sender as Santa Claus, the recipient as Tooth Fairy, and the subject as Easter Bunny."

- **Mark Exhibits**

You are responsible for making sure the court reporter and opposing counsel have access to an exhibit before you refer to it during deposition questioning. Local customs as well as whether a deposition is in-person or remote are likely to affect the process of including court reporters and opposing counsel in the pre-questioning exhibits process.

As the examining attorney, local custom may allow you to mark exhibits yourself, either before or during a deposition. (In this context, "marking the exhibit" typically means writing the number of the exhibit on a label that is then placed on the exhibit). For in-person depositions, a more common practice is to hand the document you just described to the court reporter and ask for it to be marked. For example:

> Q: I am now handing this document to the court reporter. Please mark it as Exhibit 4.

For remote depositions, handing a physical copy of a document to the court reporter or the deponent is not possible. Instead, you need to make some choices before the deposition about how to mark exhibits and show them to the deponent. Common approaches include:

- Providing the court reporter with electronic copies of all documents to be marked as exhibits prior to the deposition, and then instructing the court reporter to "screen share" each document when you want to question the deponent about it.
- Using a "screen share" option from your computer when you want to question the deponent about a document and then sending each document to the court reporter after the deposition to be included with the deposition transcript as marked exhibits.
- Sending copies of all documents to the court reporter, as well as to the deponent and their counsel, prior to the deposition and then asking the deponent to reference their copy of each exhibit at the appropriate time. (The disadvantage of this approach is that it provides the deponent and opposing counsel with a preview of the exhibits in advance of the deposition).

Once an exhibit has been marked, refer to it by its exhibit number or letter. In other words, instead of stating "the document" or "the email," refer to it consistently as "Exhibit 4."

- **Provide Copies of Exhibits**

After an exhibit has been identified and marked, you need to provide copies to both the deponent and opposing counsel before you ask any questions about the exhibit. For an in-person deposition, simply hand the marked exhibit to the deponent and copies to opposing counsel and indicate on the record that you are doing so. For example: "I am handing Exhibit 4 to the deponent, and copies of what has been marked as Exhibit 4 to counsel." If the deposition is taking place remotely, you can either send an electronic copy of the exhibit to the deponent and opposing counsel prior to the deposition or display the exhibit using a screen share function.

- **Exhibit-Related Questioning**

Now you are ready to question the deponent about the exhibit. Again, whenever you refer to an exhibit, maintain a clear record by referring to the exhibit by its number or letter rather than using potentially vague references like "this" or "the email." If your questions pertain to a specific portion of an exhibit, also specify for the record that specific portion. For example you might say:

Q: Please take a look at Exhibit 4. Drawing your attention to the last paragraph at the bottom of the page 2 of Exhibit 4, do you see the paragraph that begins, "If you do not improve. . . ."?

A: Yes.

Q: Please read that paragraph to yourself and let me know when you have had a chance to review it.

A: OK. I have read it.

You can now question the deponent about that portion of the exhibit knowing your transcript will be clear.

2. AUTHENTICATE AN EXHIBIT

To authenticate an exhibit is to elicit foundational evidence sufficient to support a conclusion that it is genuine (i.e. that the exhibit is what you claim it is).

Evidence rules allow you to use leading questions, to authenticate exhibits because the testimony pertains to a foundational matter. For example:

Q: Mr. Jordan, you have had an opportunity to review Exhibit B, correct?

A: Yes.

Q: Exhibit B is a true and correct copy of an email you sent to Mr. Allen on April 29, correct?

A: Yes.

Q: And you know Exhibit B is a copy of the email you sent to Mr. Allen because you are the person who drafted that email, correct?

A: That's right.

A deponent may not possess sufficient personal knowledge to authenticate an exhibit. In this situation, you may ask whether a deponent has any reason to doubt an exhibit's authenticity. That can help you anticipate whether your adversary will contest an exhibit's authenticity. For example:

Q: Do you have any reason to believe the signature at the bottom of Exhibit D is not Mr. Allen's signature?

A: No.

3. DIAGRAMS

Maintaining a clear record is particularly important when you ask a deponent to draw a diagram or mark up an existing exhibit. Your goal is to be clear enough to enable anyone looking at the diagram while following the deposition testimony to understand what the markings on the diagram represent. As with other exhibits, keep the transcript clear by asking the court reporter to mark the diagram as an exhibit and then consistently refer to it by exhibit number throughout your questioning.

In the example that follows, assume you have asked the deponent to draw a diagram of a room where a particular conversation took place:

Q: I am handing a blank piece of paper to the court reporter. Please mark this as Exhibit 24.

[*Court reporter marks the document as Exhibit 24*]

Q: Deponent, I hand you what has been marked as Exhibit 24 and ask you to draw a bird's eye view of the room in which you spoke to Ms. Smith last August. Do you remember the layout of the room where you and Ms. Smith met?

A: Sure. It was in her home office.

Q: OK, as best you can please prepare a sketch on Exhibit 24 that depicts the furnishings within the walls of the room.

A: I can try. OK, it looked like this.

Q: Thank you. Let the record reflect that Exhibit 24 is the deponent's sketch of the room where the meeting with Ms. Smith took place. I notice a line at the bottom of the page. Is that the door to the room?

A: Yeah, this is the door.

Q: Can you write the word "door" under that line to identify the door?

A: Sure.

Q: Thanks. Do you know how large the room was?

A: I can't say for sure.

Q: I don't need an exact measurement. Just your best estimate of how large the room was.

A: Maybe 12 feet by 10 feet.

Q: Could you write the number 12 next to each of the longer walls you drew on Exhibit 24 and the number 10 next to the shorter walls to indicate the approximate length of those walls?

A: Sure.

Q: Thanks. Now can you tell us about the furniture in the room?

A: There was a desk, a few chairs, and a bookshelf.

Q: On Exhibit 24, have you drawn the desk that was in Ms. Smith's home office?

A: Yes, it was this L-shaped desk here.

Q: Great. Please write the word "desk" inside the shape you just drew to represent where the desk was. Now, how many chairs were in the room?

A: Three. One behind the desk and two right here.

Q: OK, can you mark the chair you drew behind the desk as C1? And can you label the other chairs you drew as C2 and C3, respectively? Thanks. What is the other object in your sketch?

A: That's the bookshelf.

Q: Can you label that with a B? Great.

Q: Where were you during your conversation with Ms. Smith?

A: I was sitting on this chair.

Q: You just pointed to the chair you labeled C2, correct?

A: Yeah, sorry, I was sitting in C2 and Ms. Smith was in C1.

Q: Thanks. How far was it from where you were sitting to where Ms. Smith was sitting?

A: Maybe 5 feet.

Q: Was there anything on the desk between you and Ms. Smith?

A: She had a computer monitor here and maybe some papers over here.

Q: Can you draw the outline of the computer monitor and label it as CM? Thanks. And it looks like you drew a rectangle next to the monitor as well, was that where the papers were?

A: Yeah, there were a few stacks of paper piled up here.

Q: Can you please put a P inside that rectangle to represent where the papers were?

A: Sure. . . .

When diagrams are "dynamic," remember to account for changes in the positions of people or objects. For example, if in the illustration above Ms. Smith got up and moved from the chair to the bookshelf, maintain a clear record by asking the deponent to draw a dotted line to indicate the path she took and label it accordingly.

CHAPTER 12

MAKING AND RESPONDING TO OBJECTIONS AND INSTRUCTIONS NOT TO ANSWER

This Chapter provides an overview of the basic rules and strategies relating to making and responding to objections and instructions not to answer. It also discusses improper deposition tactics and strategies that an opposing counsel might employ and how you might respond to them.

1. MAKING OBJECTIONS

A. PURPOSE OF OBJECTIONS

FRCP 30(c)(2) provides that when an objection is made at deposition, "the examination shall proceed, with the testimony being taken subject to the objections." Consequently, subject to the three exceptions discussed below, deposition objections do not prevent deponents from having to answer questions.

As a result, you generally object in order to "preserve" objections to a later time when your adversary attempts to offer the deposition testimony into evidence at trial or use it to support a pre-trial motion. As discussed in the following subsection, some objections—commonly known as "curable" objections—must be made during the deposition or you will waive your right to object at the time of trial or in connection with a motion. Other objections—commonly known as "non-curable" objections—can be raised for the first time at trial or in connection with a motion.

B. "CURABLE" AND "NON-CURABLE" OBJECTIONS

As a general rule, judges consider an objection to be "curable" if through further questions deposing counsel could have obviated the evidentiary problem raised by an objection. On the other hand, objections that cannot be overcome through further questioning are preserved and can be raised for the first time at trial or in connection with a motion.

Whether an objection is curable is an issue that can't be fully addressed in the abstract. The reason is that curability depends not only on the ground for objection, but also on the unique legal and factual issues of individual cases. However, for your general guidance, Section "a" below identifies common "use them or lose them" objections that you'll probably waive if you don't make at deposition. As you'll see, most "curable" objections involve the form of questions rather than their content. Section "b" identifies a second set of common objections to questions that typically cannot be cured and so are likely to be preserved even though you don't make them at deposition.

1. Objections That Commonly Are Curable

The following objections are ones which you typically must make at deposition or waive the ability to assert later. The "possible cures" that the examples include demonstrate that your objection does afford an adversary a realistic opportunity to fix the evidentiary failings.[1]

- **Compound**

A question is compound because it is essentially two questions phrased as one.

- Example: "Who was at the party and which of them had you met previously?"
- Possible Cure: Divide the question into two or more smaller questions, e.g. "Who was at the party?" and "Which of them had you met previously?"

- **Vague**

A question is vague when a deponent cannot be reasonably certain of the information being sought.

- Example: "Before that meeting, what was going on between you and Mr. Pell?" Here, a deponent may reasonably be uncertain about the meaning of the phrase "what was going on."
- Possible Cure: "What did you and Mr. Pell discuss prior to the meeting?" (The "cure seeks a response about a discrete topic.)

---

[1] This section does not discuss objections based on privilege. If you contend that a question seeks information that is privileged, you should both raise the privilege objection and also instruct the deponent not to answer the question.

- **Assumes Facts Not in Evidence**

A question assumes facts not in evidence when it incorporates information to which a deponent has not testified.

- Example: A deponent who has not testified to talking to a Mr. Pell prior to a meeting is asked: "When you and Mr. Pell met before the termination meeting, what did you talk about?"
- Possible Cure: Ask a question that establishes the assumed fact: "Did you and Mr. Pell meet before the termination meeting?"

- **Leading**

A leading question is one which either by its wording or through the questioner's tone of voice suggests the answer the deponent should give. If deposing counsel is deposing your client, a witness "identified with your client" or a "hostile witness," you should not object on this ground since leading questions are permitted with such witnesses.[2] If the deponent is a neutral witness, leading questions are usually improper and you might object.

- Example: "Isn't it true that you met with Mr. Pell before the meeting?"

---

[2] FRE 611(c). When you are unsure if the deponent is "identified with your client" or "hostile" toward deposing counsel or his client, you may decide to make leading objections to avoid a waiver.

- Possible Cure: "Had you met Mr. Pell before you went to the meeting?"

- **Misquotes or Mischaracterizes Testimony**

This objection arises when a questioner inaccurately summarizes or refers to a deponent's earlier testimony.

- Example: Your adversary asks a deponent who had testified that your client, Ms. Anderson, "shouted" during a performance review: "When Ms. Anderson raised her voice during the performance review, do you think anyone outside your office could have heard what Ms. Anderson said to you at that time?"

- Possible Cure 1: Restate the question and correct the mischaracterization: "When Ms. Anderson allegedly shouted during the performance review. . ."

- Possible Cure 2: Delete the reference to the prior testimony: "During the performance review, do you think anyone outside your office could have heard what Ms. Anderson said to you at that time?"

- **Calls for a Narrative**

A question "calls for a narrative" when it is so broad in scope that opposing counsel cannot anticipate the limits of an answer.

- Example: "Please tell me everything that happened after you got to the intersection."

- Possible Cure: "What did you see when you first got to the intersection."

- **Argumentative**

An argumentative question asserts a questioner's argument or comments on testimony in the form of a question.

- Example: "Since Mrs. Green's report was written right after the meeting, why shouldn't we believe Mrs. Green's report rather than your testimony?"
- Possible Cure: "Why do you think that Ms. Green's report is inaccurate?"

- **Lack of Personal Knowledge/Lack of Foundation**

These objections are appropriate when the record does not indicate that a deponent had first-hand knowledge.

- Example: The adversary asks, "What did Ms. Julian do after she left the meeting?" However, the record doesn't indicate that the deponent was in a position to know what Ms. Julian did after she left the meeting.
- Possible Cure: Establish the deponent's personal knowledge: "Did you see Ms. Julian after she left the meeting?"

- **Calls for Speculation**

This objection is similar to the objection for lack of personal knowledge. The objection is appropriate when the question asks a deponent to testify about a matter which the deponent would appear to have no basis for knowing.

- Example: Your adversary asks, "Why was Ms. Julian worried about the decision to purchase computers?" The question calls for speculation because a deponent cannot perceive another's thoughts.

- Possible Cure: Establish the deponent's personal knowledge: "Did Ms. Julian tell you what she thought about the decision to purchase computers?"

- **Inadmissible Opinion**

This objection usually asserts that an opinion is (a) not rationally based on the deponent's perceptions or (b) not helpful to a clear understanding of the deponent's testimony.

- Example: A deponent who testified that "I caught a quick glimpse of the driver" is asked, "Did the driver appear to be driving carefully?" (In this example, a "quick glimpse" suggests that the opinion may not be rationally based on the deponent's perceptions.)

- Possible Cure: Establish that the deponent has an adequate basis for the opinion: "How long did you watch the driver?" "Over what distance?"

This objection can also raise the issue of whether a question calls for an expert opinion from a witness who has not been qualified as an expert. Your adversary can cure this problem by qualifying the deponent as an expert.

- **Privilege**

Objections based on a privilege (e.g. attorney client, work product, etc.) must be made at deposition or they are waived.

2. Common "Incurable" Objections That You Can Raise Later Even if You Don't Make Them at Deposition

The following objections generally cannot be cured by deposing counsel at deposition. Consequently, you can raise them later even if you don't make them at deposition.

- **Inadmissible Legal Conclusion**

If a question asks for an improper legal conclusion, your adversary can't cure the problem through further questioning. Hence, the objection is preserved even if you don't make it.

- **Irrelevant**

Typically, your adversary can do nothing to cure this objection; evidence is either relevant or it is not, depending on the contentions at the time your adversary seeks to use the evidence. Hence, you usually need not make relevance objections at deposition. There may be some circumstances, however, where additional questions would demonstrate relevance.

- **Hearsay**

Generally, hearsay objections cannot be cured by rewording the question and therefore hearsay objections ordinarily need not be made at a deposition. There may be circumstances, however where the objection can be cured with foundational questions that establish the grounds for a hearsay exception or exemption.

- Example: Your adversary asks a deponent who saw an automobile accident, "What did the passenger in the defendant's car say when you first went over to the car?"
- Possible Cure: Elicit foundational evidence establishing that the passenger's statement falls within the "excited utterance" exception to the hearsay rule: "How long after the collision did you speak to the passenger?" "What was the passenger's demeanor at the time you spoke to the passenger?"

C. FORGOING OBJECTIONS

You needn't object at every valid opportunity. For example, it makes sense to forgo objecting when an answer is obviously helpful to you, or if a topic is trivial. More subtly, you may forgo a legitimate objection to prevent deposing counsel from inquiring into an area that hurts your case. For example, making a "lacks foundation" objection may cause opposing counsel to ask more extensive background questions about a topic that would bring out details that are harmful to your client.

D. PHRASING OBJECTIONS PROPERLY

If objections are to give fair notice to deposing counsel as to curable evidentiary problems, it follows that to object properly you should identify your ground or grounds for objection. FRCP 30(d)(1) also requires that objections at deposition be stated "concisely and in a non-argumentative and non-suggestive manner." Thus, your objections need and should refer only to their legal basis or bases.[3] For example:

- "Objection. Hearsay."
- "Objection. Lack of foundation, lack of personal knowledge, inadmissible opinion and calls for speculation."
- "Objection. The question is compound."
- "Objection. The question assumes facts not in evidence."

Avoid "speaking" objections, i.e., objections that include both a legal ground for objection and argument. Such speaking objections violate FRCP 30(d)(1) because they disrupt a deposition and/or "coach" a deponent by suggesting how the deponent should respond to a question. Speaking objections are discussed in more detail in section 3 below.

---

[3] Note that in some jurisdictions, however, the practice is not to identify the legal basis for the objection, but only to state that the objection is to the form of the question.

2. RESPONDING TO OBJECTIONS

The following subsections set forth strategies for responding to opposing counsels' objections.

STEP ONE: OBTAIN AN ANSWER

Your usual initial response to an objection to your question should be to obtain an answer. Whether or not an objection is valid, you are almost always entitled to an answer. This result follows from FRCP 30(c), which provides that when an objection is made at deposition, the examination proceeds with testimony taken subject to the objection. Because testimony is taken subject to objections, the court need not rule on the validity of objections made at deposition until after the deposition is complete. This approach saves a great deal of time and money because deposing counsel does not have to run to court to get a ruling on every objection in order to obtain an answer.

As a result, you may respond to an objection as follows:

1. Q: Who are the people who own stock in the Wiltern Corporation?

2. Opposing Counsel: Objection. Irrelevant and not proportional to the needs of the case.

3. Q: Will you answer the question please?

4. A: Well, I own some and. . .

The general rule, "obtain answers even in the face of valid objections," is of course subject to common sense exceptions. If you can easily reword a question without altering its meaning, or if you realize that a question is hopelessly ambiguous or confusing, you can keep the record clear by simply withdrawing the question and rephrasing it.

STEP TWO: DECIDE WHETHER THE OBJECTION IS VALID

Because failure to cure a problem raised by a valid objection can prevent your using deposition testimony later in the case, after obtaining an answer, you should generally evaluate the objection's validity and determine whether a judge would likely sustain the objection.

If you are comfortable that an objection is obviously invalid, you may safely ignore it and proceed with further questioning. But if you think that a judge might uphold an objection, you need to think about finding a cure that can make a deposition answer available for use in support of a motion or at trial.

STEP THREE: RESPOND TO CURABLE OBJECTIONS

As discussed at the beginning of this chapter, each potentially valid objection may be cured in various ways. However, often you can use the deponent's testimony you obtained in step one to help cure the objection. For example:

1. Q: What was the next thing that happened after the October meeting with plaintiff?

2. A: We left the meeting and went out to her car.

3. Q: Then what?

4. Opposing Counsel: Objection. Vague.

5. Q: Go ahead and answer the question.

6. A: We drove home.

7. Q: So the next thing that you did after leaving the meeting and going out to her car was drive home?

8. A: Yes.

The question at No. 3 is vague because it is unclear what was being asked—there is no clear frame of reference contained in the question. But by obtaining an answer at No. 6, the attorney was able to use that information when curing the objection with question No. 7.

3. INSTRUCTIONS NOT TO ANSWER

You can properly instruct a deponent not to answer a question only in one or more of the following circumstances:

- Deposing counsel's question calls for information protected by a recognized privilege,[4]
- Deposing counsel's question violates a prior court ordered limitation on discovery, or
- You are suspending the deposition to seek a protective order because deposing counsel is

---

[4] FRCP 30(c) uses only the term privilege, but courts generally interpret the term to include work product.

conducting the deposition in bad faith or in such manner as unreasonably to annoy, embarrass, or oppress the deponent or a party.

4. RESPONDING TO INVALID INSTRUCTIONS NOT TO ANSWER

Only by going to court and obtaining an "Order to Compel Answers" can you compel an answer from a deponent who refuses to answer a question pursuant to opposing counsel's improper instruction. However, the following steps may enable you to obtain an answer without the delay and expense of seeking such an order. And if you do have to make a motion to compel an answer, these steps increase the likelihood that a judge will grant your motion and sanction your adversary.

A. ON THE RECORD, ASK YOUR ADVERSARY TO WITHDRAW THE INSTRUCTION

The best first step to obtaining an answer is to indicate on the record why you believe that opposing counsel has no proper basis for issuing the instruction. For example, if opposing counsel instructed the deponent not to answer on the ground of privilege, respond by pointing out politely why the information you seek is not privileged. The FRCP require that you confer or attempt to confer in good faith with opposing counsel to try to secure answers before seeking a court order compelling an answer. Your politely pointing out the error of opposing counsel's ways constitutes partial compliance with this requirement.

B. PUT THE DEPONENT'S REFUSAL TO ANSWER ON THE RECORD

If your adversary continues to instruct the deponent not to answer, place the deponent's refusal to answer on the record. One way to do this is to ask the court reporter to repeat the question and then ask the deponent, "Do you refuse to answer that question?" and "Is your refusal to answer based on the advice of counsel?"

C. DETERMINE THE SCOPE OF THE INSTRUCTION NOT TO ANSWER

Follow up a refusal to answer with additional questions that relate to the subject matter of the question that the deponent refused to answer.

If opposing counsel instructs the deponent not to answer the additional questions and you later seek a court order compelling answers, a single motion can encompass all the questions that the deponent refused to answer. The additional questions indicate the scope of your inquiry, making it likely that any court order you obtain will be broad enough to elicit the information you're seeking. Moreover, the additional questions may allow opposing counsel to make a graceful retreat. Opposing counsel can choose not to object to the additional questions, allowing you to obtain the information you want while not causing opposing counsel to lose face in front of a client by having to withdraw a previously given instruction.

The following examples illustrate the above strategies for responding when opposing counsel improperly instructs a deponent not to answer.

Example 1 (Responding to an Instruction Based on an Invalid Claim of Work Product Privilege)

In a case involving the crash of a small commuter airplane, you are counsel for plaintiff and are deposing Ms. Herman, the airline employee who investigated the accident. The deposition proceeds as follows:

1. Q: Ms. Herman, after the accident, did you obtain witness statements from any of the plane's passengers?

2. Opposing Counsel: Objection. Work product privilege. I instruct her not to answer.

3. Q: Counsel, my question merely asks about the existence of a statement. It does not go to the content of any statement and therefore the work product privilege does not apply.

4. Opposing Counsel: I'm still instructing the witness not to answer.

5. Q: Counsel, can you please spell out your basis for saying that work product applies in these circumstances? That's required by FRCP 26 (b)(5).

6. Opposing Counsel: I'm instructing the witness not to answer because her investigation after the accident is covered by work product in

that she was assigned to investigate the accident by the airline.

7. Q: Ms. Herman, on the basis of counsel's instructions are you refusing to answer my question about whether, after the accident, you obtained witness statements from any of the plane's passengers?

8. A: Yes I am.

9. Q: After the accident, did you talk with any of the plane's passengers?

10. Opposing Counsel: I instruct you not to answer on the grounds of work product.

11. Q: Ms. Herman, on the basis of counsel's instructions are you refusing to answer my question about whether, after the accident, you talked with any of the plane's passengers?

12. A: Yes I am.

13. Q: After the accident what are the names, if any, of the plane's passengers with whom you had conversations?

14. Opposing Counsel: Same instruction on the same ground.

15. Q: Ms. Herman on the basis of counsel's instructions are you refusing to answer my question about what are the names of any of the plane's passengers with whom you had conversations after the accident?

16. A: Yes I am.

17. Q: While you were investigating the accident, did you see any evidence indicating that there was a fire on the plane before it crashed?

18. Opposing Counsel: Same instruction on the same ground.

19. Q: Ms. Herman, on the basis of counsel's instructions are you refusing to answer my question about whether, while you were investigating the accident, you saw any evidence indicating that there was a fire on the plane before it crashed?

20. A: Yes I am.

In No. 3, you try to get the adversary to withdraw the instruction by explaining why the instruction is improper. In No. 5, you remind opposing counsel of the obligation to spell out the facts indicating that the privilege applies. In Nos. 9, 13, and 17, you ask additional questions pertaining to the subject matter you intend to pursue. In Nos. 7, 11, 15 and 19, you make sure that the record explicitly indicates that the deponent refuses to answer based on advice of counsel.

<u>Example 2</u> (Responding to an Improper Instruction Based on Claim Other than Privilege)

Your adversary may issue improper instructions not to answer on grounds other than privilege. For example, opposing counsel may object and instruct a deponent not to answer on the ground that your question is vague, calls for information that is irrelevant or not proportional to the needs of the case, calls for an inadmissible opinion or speculation, has been asked and answered, etc. Even though objections on such grounds may be valid, they cannot justify an instruction not to answer if the questions don't seek privileged information or violate a court order. And you may respond to these improper instructions just as you do to instructions based on an illegitimate claim of privilege. Consider the following illustrative example:

1. Q: Mr. Foster, who owns stock in the Wiltern Corporation?

2. Opposing Counsel: Objection. That's irrelevant. This case isn't about the shareholders, it's about whether the Wiltern Corporation is liable for what you allege was a defective product. I instruct the witness not to answer.

3. Q: Counsel, as I'm sure you know, you are not authorized to instruct the witness not to answer unless my question calls for privileged information seeks information subject to a protective order, or unless you are terminating the deposition to seek a protective order. That's the rule stated in 30(d)(1) of the FRCP. I have a copy of the rule right here if you and your client would like to look at it. Since my question clearly doesn't call for privileged information and isn't subject to a protective order, I'm entitled to have an answer unless you are going to terminate the

deposition to seek a protective order. Otherwise, the witness should answer and, if necessary, the court can rule later on whether your objection is well taken.

4. Opposing Counsel: That's your interpretation of the rules. I'm still instructing the witness not to answer unless you can explain to me why this information is relevant.

5. Q: Counsel, I'm not obligated to explain the legal theory on which my question is based in order to get an answer. However, if Mr. Foster or any of his friends or family own a substantial amount of stock in the Wiltern, they may suffer financial loss as a result of this case, and that may go to bias.

6. Opposing Counsel: I'm still instructing the witness not to answer.

7. Q [To Reporter]: Would you read back the pending question please? [Question is read back.] Mr. Foster, on the basis of counsel's instructions are you refusing to answer that question?

8. A: Yes I am.

9. Q: Mr. Foster, let me make my inquiry a bit narrower. Do you own any stock in the Wiltern Corporation?

10. A: Yes. I own about 80% of the stock.

11. Q: And does anyone in your family, other than you, own any stock in the corporation?

12. A: Yes. My brother owns about 10% and. . .

In this example, you first explain why the instruction is improper (No. 3). When you fail to persuade opposing counsel to withdraw the instruction, you provide a brief explanation of why the question is proper (No. 5). As you indicate, you are not required to provide this explanation, but doing so may persuade an opponent to withdraw the instruction.[5] When the instruction still stands (as it does in this example at No. 6), you put the deponent's refusal to answer on the record (Nos. 7 and 8). Then you go on with additional questions in the same subject area (Nos. 9–12). If as happens in this example the deponent is allowed to answer these questions, you've obtained the desired information while allowing opposing counsel to "save face" by not having to explicitly withdraw the instruction not to answer in front of the client. Of course, had opposing counsel instructed the deponent not to answer any questions pertaining to stock ownership, you would have to either move to compel or forgo this information.

D. OBTAIN AN ORDER COMPELLING AN ANSWER

If opposing counsel continues to refuse to withdraw an improper instruction not to answer, and you still want answers to your questions, you may

---

[5] The downside of an explanation is possibly educating the witness or opposing counsel about your legal strategies.

- Suspend a deposition immediately and move for an order to compel answers; or
- Complete your deposition questioning on all matters except those that the deponent has refused to answer, and then suspend the deposition and seek an order to compel answers.

If you choose the first alternative, a deposition may proceed as follows:

1. Q [To Reporter]: Would you read back the pending question please? [Question is read back] Mr. Foster, on the basis of counsel's instructions are you refusing to answer that question?

2. A: Yes I am.

3. Q: Counsel, if you do not withdraw the instruction not to answer, I will suspend the deposition at once and move the court for an order compelling the deponent to answer.

4. Opposing Counsel: My instruction not to answer stands.

5. Q: Very well. I have not finished questioning your client, but at this time I am suspending the deposition to seek an order compelling your client to answer the questions he has refused to answer at this deposition.

You would follow up with a motion for an order compelling the deponent to answer and for sanctions against your opponent.

This first alternative has its downsides. You commit to the time and expense of a motion to compel. And you must wait until the deposition resumes to obtain the remainder of the deponent's testimony.

If you conclude deposition questioning on matters other than those the deponent has refused to answer, you can then indicate on the record that you are reserving the right to move to compel with respect to questions the deponent has refused to answer, and necessary follow-up questions. You can then later decide if the withheld information is sufficiently important to justify the time and expense of seeking a court order.

Court rules in many jurisdictions offer a third and far less costly and complicated alternative. A judge (or magistrate) may be available online or by telephone to resolve disputes relating to instructions not to answer. In these jurisdictions, you recess a deposition and contact a judge (or magistrate). After the court reporter reads the questions to which the dispute pertains, both counsel can be heard on the propriety of the instructions not to answer. If the judge or magistrate issues a ruling "on the spot" the deposition can resume immediately.

5. RESPONDING TO INAPPROPRIATE BEHAVIOR BY OPPOSING COUNSEL

Though deposition practices should mirror those at trial, that is, attorneys should behave equally professionally during depositions and court proceedings, opposing counsel may conduct themselves during depositions in ways that clearly would not be tolerated at trial.

- **Argumentative Objections**

For example, instead of concisely identifying a legal basis for an objection opposing counsel may resort to an improper argumentative objection.

Example

Objection. Irrelevant. You're never going to use that sort of information at trial. You're just wasting our time. Focus on the facts of the case, why don't you. If you want to go on a fishing expedition, do it on your own time and not ours. We've been here too long already, and now you're going into this stuff. My client and I will only stay here one more hour, and then we're leaving. So why don't you ask something having to do with the facts of this case?

Another form of improper disruptive behavior is to use an objection to ask for your strategic goals.

Example

Objection. I don't see how this is relevant, counsel. I'll be happy to have the deponent answer the question if you'll explain why this information is or might be relevant to the case.

You are under no obligation to share your theories of the case with opposing counsel so you can simply ask the deponent to answer your question (unless counsel instructs the deponent not to answer, in which case, see section 1(A) above).

- **Improper Coaching**

"Witness coaching" comprises a variety of methods by which an opposing attorney may seek to influence a deponent's testimony. For example, an attorney may use a "speaking objection" to suggest an answer to a deponent:

Example

Counsel, you're asking the witness to recall a conversation that took place months ago. You can't expect her to tell you the exact words that were used.

You can try to combat this impropriety by objecting on the record, asking counsel to confine remarks to proper objections, and if necessary adjourn a deposition and seek sanctions from a court.

Another example of improper coaching is through whispered conferences. Opposing counsel cannot confer with a deponent when a question is pending. If you suspect that counsel is attempting to coach the witness with such tactics, you might state for the record that counsel is conferring with the witness. Ultimately, you have to decide if the problem is serious enough to suspend the deposition and move for a protective order prohibiting such conferences. Visually recording depositions is a useful method of discouraging attorneys from conferring with deponents.

Similarly, an attorney may try to improperly coach the deponent by asking for a recess when a question is pending. In a deposition of any length, defending counsel will routinely and properly call for recesses to allow the participants to relax and re-charge. Defending attorneys commonly and properly use these recesses to review testimony with deponents and to remind them of important facts. But a request for a break when a question is pending, or when you are in the middle of an important line of questioning may constitute an improper attempt at coaching. Your options are limited; you cannot physically or electronically stop them from taking a break. You can note for the record your objection to the recess and indicate any factors suggesting that opposing counsel requested the recess in order to instruct the deponent as to how to respond to your questions: "I'd like the record to reflect that this is the third time counsel has asked for a recess when a question was pending." In the case of serious and repeated abuse of conferences, you may suspend the deposition and seek a protective order and sanctions.

6. A CAUTIONARY NOTE ABOUT PROTECTIVE ORDERS

The issuance of a protective order is within a court's nearly unfettered discretion. Even if you've fulfilled all the preconditions for a protective order (e.g., you've made a good faith effort to resolve the dispute), you may need to demonstrate that opposing counsel's behavior is a serious, and not merely a technical, violation of the rules. Although FRCP 30(c) provides that examination at deposition should proceed generally as at trial, no judge is present at a deposition to mediate disputes between counsel. Moreover, judges recognize that disputes are common because it is natural for opposing counsel to want to appear protective of their clients, especially in the face of legitimate but sometimes damaging, uncomfortable, and arguably repetitive, cross examination. These disputes, and the understandable tension that accompanies them, often result in at least technical violations of deposition rules. Courts would be swamped if every violation resulted in a motion for a protective order. Consequently, when you seek a protective order, you should be prepared to demonstrate that opposing counsel's behavior has materially affected your legitimate discovery efforts.

Finally, your ability to obtain a protective order and/or sanctions against opposing counsel may well depend on the propriety of your own deposition behavior. Respond to opposing counsel and question the deponent as you would if a judge were present. You can be professional and courteous and still be a zealous advocate. And maintaining a professional demeanor can improve your chances of success should a judge have occasion to examine a deposition transcript or visual recording in connection with a motion for a protective order.

CHAPTER 13

FRCP 30(b)(6) "SUBJECT MATTER" DEPOSITIONS

FRCP 30(b)(6) allows you to depose a corporation, a partnership, an association or a government agency on one or more subjects without identifying a particular person to be deposed. When you notice a 30(b)(6) "subject matter" deposition, an entity must respond by designating for deposition one or more representatives who are most knowledgeable about the subjects set forth in your notice. When a designee testifies, the answers are binding on an entity to the same extent that deposition testimony of an individual is binding on that person. This Chapter explores the noticing and taking of subject matter depositions.

1. WHY TAKE A SUBJECT MATTER DEPOSITION?

Subject matter depositions often reduce discovery efforts and costs. You can avoid the time and expense of first sending out interrogatories to identify entity representatives who are knowledgeable about a relevant subject, and then deposing each of those people. Instead, you can simply require the entity to produce the person(s) most knowledgeable in response to a single deposition notice. Thus, for example, in litigation about a plane crash you might send a 30(b)(6) notice to the airline requiring it to produce the person(s) most knowledgeable about subjects such as the maintenance history of the plane and the electrical system on the plane.

Subject matter depositions can also help you educate yourself about an entity's organizational structure, procedures and operations. Assume for example that you want to learn about a financial entity's usual practices and procedures when initiating a foreclosure. You can notice a subject matter deposition on this subject and educate yourself about what usually happens, and then later take additional depositions to determine what actually happened in your client's case.

2. HOW MANY 30(b)(6) DEPOSITIONS CAN YOU TAKE?

You may be limited to one 30(b)(6) deposition for a given entity. The reason is that the person being deposed is the entity, and under FRCP 30(a)(2), in the absence of court permission, you can depose a person only once.

3. THE IMPORTANCE OF COMPREHENSIVE 30(b)(6) NOTICES

Since you may be limited to a single FRCP 30(b)(6) deposition, frame a notice comprehensively so as to include all discoverable subjects that interest you. It is not necessary that a single person within an organization be knowledgeable about all the subjects you identify. Rather, an entity is responsible for designating and producing representatives who can testify fully on each subject in a notice Therefore, if no single person within an entity is knowledgeable on all subjects in a notice, the entity must designate as many persons as are necessary to produce a knowledgeable person on each subject. If an entity fails to designate a person who is knowledgeable about a discoverable subject included in your notice, you are entitled to a court order requiring an entity to produce a knowledgeable person and possibly to sanctions.

4. QUESTIONING 30(b)(6) DESIGNEES

The subsections below explore two questioning concerns that tend to be unique to 30(b)(6) depositions.

A. IS THE DESIGNEE KNOWLEDGEABLE?

To avoid wasting time questioning a designee who in reality has little information about subjects in a 30(b)(6) notice, determine the extent of a designee's knowledge at a deposition's outset. To do so, you might pursue topics such as the following:

- Is the designee the most knowledgeable person within the entity regarding the topics identified in the deposition notice.
- Who else within the entity might be as knowledgeable or more knowledgeable than the designee on each topic?
- What makes the designee knowledgeable about the topics identified in the deposition notice?

- What did the designee do to prepare to testify on each topic? For example, what materials did a designee look at and with whom did the designee talk?

Exploring such topics can help you determine whether an entity has properly complied with the requirement that it produce a person who can testify fully about the subjects in your notice. You also gain an indication at the outset of the extent to which a designee will testify from personal knowledge.[1] You may also identify materials of which you were previously unaware and ask to see them before questioning the designee.

In the example below, you probe the designee's knowledge by using the deposition notice and proceeding through the subjects it includes.

1. Q: Mr. Montross, I'd like to show you this four-page document entitled Notice of Deposition that has been marked as Exhibit 1. Will you look at it please?

2. A: OK.

3. Q: Have you seen a copy of Exhibit 1 before coming here today?

---

[1] There is no requirement that a designee only testify from personal knowledge. Indeed, in some instances an entity may no longer have in its employ persons who are personally knowledgeable on the subjects in your notice. However, if the designee is not personally knowledgeable you want to know that such is the situation. In addition, you want to identify who is personally knowledgeable so that you can decide whether you also want to depose that person.

4. A: Yes.

5. Q: When did you first see it?

6. A: About a week ago.

7. Q: Where did you see Exhibit 1?

8. A: In my lawyer's office.

9. Q: Was anyone else present when you saw Exhibit 1 other than your lawyer?

10. A: No.

11. Q: Please read to yourself paragraph one on page two of Exhibit 1.

12. Q: Are you knowledgeable about the topic described in paragraph one on page two of Exhibit 1?

13. A: Yes.

14. Q: What makes you knowledgeable about the topic described in paragraph one?

15. A: I was employed by Blue Bus Company as a chief mechanic for 10 years.

16. Q: What else makes you knowledgeable with respect to the topic described in paragraph one on page two of Exhibit 1?

17. A: I worked on and inspected brakes for the company during that time period and I supervised the work of other mechanics who worked on the brakes.

18. Q: Is there anything else that makes you knowledgeable about the topic described in paragraph one on page two of Exhibit 1?

19. A: No.

20. Q: Did you read or review any materials in preparing to testify about the topic described in paragraph one on page two of Exhibit 1?

21. A: No.

22. Q: Are you aware of any written or electronic materials relating to the topic described in paragraph one on page two of Exhibit 1?

23. A: A company online manual sets forth how often we should inspect the brakes of company buses and there are various online manufacturers' manuals on brake maintenance and repair.

24. Q: Are there any other materials relating to the topic described in paragraph one on page two of Exhibit 1?

25. A: Not that I can think of at this time.

26. Q: If you wanted to find out if Blue Bus Company had any other materials relating to the topic described in paragraph one on page two of Exhibit 1, how would you go about doing so?

27. A: I'd ask our maintenance supervisor, Robert Garcia.

28. Q: In preparing to testify today, why didn't you read the company manual that sets forth how often the brakes of company buses should be inspected?

29. A: Because I'm quite familiar with it and because we have a vehicle database that we use constantly to remind ourselves of when inspections on each company vehicle need to be done.

30. Q: Any other reason you didn't read the manual?

31. A: No.

32. Q: Please describe the vehicle database.

33. A: [Answer omitted]

34. Q: Is there anyone at the Blue Bus Company who you believe knows more than you do about the topic described in paragraph one on page two of Exhibit 1?

35. A: Mr. Garcia may know more than I do; I'm not sure on that point.

36. Q: Anyone else beside Mr. Garcia?

37. A: Well, Marshall Fogerty, but he is no longer with the company. He retired about two months ago.

38. Q: Why do you believe that Mr. Fogerty might be more knowledgeable on the topic in paragraph one on page two of Exhibit 1?

39. A: He was the overall maintenance supervisor for more than twenty years.

40. Q: Do you know how to contact Mr. Fogerty?

41. A: No, but I believe Mr. Garcia knows how to get hold of him.

You would then ask a similar set of questions for each of the topics identified in the deposition notice.

B. INQUIRE ABOUT AN ENTITY'S ACTIONS RATHER THAN A DESIGNEE'S

When you question a designee, an ultimate goal is to obtain information about the entity and its operations and to bind the entity to the designee's statements about the entity. Therefore, ask about the entity and not the designee.

<u>Example</u>

<u>Incorrect</u>: How often did **you** inspect the brake systems of the buses on Route 21?

<u>Correct</u>: How often did the **Blue Bus Company** inspect the brake systems of the buses on Route 21?

When you find out what an entity has done, you can then inquire about who acted on the entity's behalf, what each individual (including the designee) did, and the foundation for the designee's knowledge.

5. GOING BEYOND THE SUBJECTS IN A NOTICE

The scope of 30(b)(6) questioning is not necessarily limited to the subjects set forth in a deposition notice.

Questioning beyond the subjects in the notice of deposition may not bind the entity. An entity that has not been notified in advance that you will pursue a subject beyond those in the notice may argue that it has not had an opportunity to designate the most knowledgeable person on the unnoticed subject, and that as a result it should not be bound by the designee's testimony.

There is also a risk that opposing counsel may take the position that when you ask questions that are outside the scope of the deposition notice, you are now taking the deposition of the individual who was designated to testify on behalf of the entity rather than deposing the entity, and that you are now using your one opportunity to depose that individual. This is another reason why you want to draft a sufficiently broad set of topics in your deposition notice.

6. CAN YOU DEPOSE A 30(b)(6) DESIGNEE TWICE?

You must ordinarily obtain court permission to depose the same person more than once. However, a 30(b)(6) designee appears on behalf of an entity and not as an individual. Therefore, the one deposition rule may not foreclose you from subsequently deposing, without court permission, an individual who has previously been designated in response to a

30(b)(6) notice. In other words, you may be able to depose the same person as a designated representative and later as an individual.

For example, assume that you send a 30(b)(6) notice to the Blue Bus Company requiring it to designate a person to be deposed regarding its general practices and procedures for maintaining the brakes on its buses. The company designates a representative who both knows about the Company's general maintenance practices and who worked on the bus involved in the accident that injured your client. If you limit your questions at the 30(b)(6) deposition to the Company's general practices, you may then be entitled to depose the designee a second time in his individual capacity to determine what he did with respect to the bus involved in the accident. On the other hand, assume at the 30(b)(6) deposition you ask both about the company's general practices and what the deponent did with respect to the bus involved in the accident. You would then arguably be questioning the deponent in his individual capacity and therefore you may not be able to depose him a second time without leave of court. Consequently, if you go beyond the scope of the matters stated in a 30(b)(6) deposition notice and question the deponent thoroughly; you may not have an opportunity for a second bite at the apple.

7. USING A 30(b)(6) DEPOSITION TO OBTAIN THE BASES FOR AN ADVERSE PARTY'S LEGAL CONTENTIONS

Special concerns arise when you use a 30(b)(6) deposition to obtain information about an adverse party's legal contentions. You should generally not phrase a 30(b)(6) notice in a way that asks an adversary to designate a person who is most knowledgeable about the facts supporting a legal theory or a legal conclusion in a pleading. For example, in litigation resulting from the crash of an airliner, assume that the airline's answer asserts that the crash resulted from the negligence of air traffic controllers. You send out a 30(b)(6) notice asking the airline to designate the "representative who is most knowledgeable about the affirmative defense in your answer that the crash was due in part to the negligence of air traffic controllers." A court might well uphold the airline's request for a protective order preventing the deposition from going forward on the ground that your deposition is an impermissible attempt to require the airline to marshal evidence supporting a legal theory.

Nevertheless, by carefully phrasing a 30(b)(6) deposition notice you may be able to depose the person most knowledgeable about the information supporting an adversary's legal contentions. In the above example, for instance, you may be able to send out a 30(b)(6) notice asking the airline to designate the "representative who is most knowledgeable about the activities of the air traffic controllers on the day of the accident giving rise to this litigation." This notice does not mention any legal theory or allegation in the pleadings. It simply seeks the person most knowledgeable about what happened on the day of the accident. Therefore, the notice is less likely to be seen as an impermissible attempt to require the airline to marshal evidence supporting a legal theory.

CHAPTER 14

"PRACTICES AND POLICIES" QUESTIONING STRATEGIES

This Chapter explores strategies for inquiring about an adverse organization's practices and policies.[1] You might confine a deposition to an organization's practices and policies, or you might ask about practices and policies as well as inquiring into the events of your specific case. For example, assume that you represent the plaintiff in an action to recover damages against a bank for failure to fund a loan. You might choose to devote an entire deposition to the bank's general policies for investigating and approving loans.[2] Alternatively, you might inquire into those matters during a deposition in which you also question a bank officer concerning the loan made to your client. Whichever option you choose, you can enhance the effectiveness of practice and policy inquiries by using the strategies discussed in this Chapter.

---

1 The term organization refers to any public or private corporation, partnership, association or agency. In some cases, you may inquire about the practices and policies of an individual rather than an organization. For example, you might make such an inquiry in a case involving a business operated by an individual.

2 You may follow the procedures outlined in FRCP 30(b)(6) when you want to take a "practice and policy" deposition but do not know which of an entity's representatives would be most knowledgeable. For more information about FRCP 30(b)(6), see Chapter 13.

1. DISTINGUISHING "PRACTICES" FROM "POLICIES"

As you'll see below, questioning strategies vary somewhat depending on whether your inquiry concerns a practice or a policy. Therefore, having in mind how a practice tends to differ from a policy may help you apply the strategies described below.

A "practice" consists of the usual series of steps that an organization or individual actually takes when processing a particular type of matter. That is, a practice consists of "what's on the ground" as part of an organization's daily operations. For instance, a practice might consist of the steps that a company usually follows when moving to terminate employees, or the procedures that a government benefits office normally follows when determining whether clients remain eligible for housing subsidies.

The term "policy" generally refers to a rule or a custom that an organization's representatives are supposed to follow when they handle a particular kind of matter. For example, a policy might be a company rule defining the type of misconduct for which employees can be terminated or a policy might set forth the steps that a company's representative **should** follow when terminating employees for certain types of misconduct. Policies may be reflected either by written materials or by unwritten customs.

2. PURPOSES OF PRACTICE AND POLICY INQUIRIES

As stated above, the usual purpose of practice and policy inquiries is not to investigate what happened in a particular case, but rather to gather information about what usually happens in a given class of cases. You might want to undertake such an inquiry for one or more of the following purposes:

Ascertaining whether practices were adhered to. Liability may turn on whether an entity or individual adhered to its usual practices when carrying out a particular action. For example, a conclusion that an employee was "wrongfully" terminated may turn in part on whether the employer diverged from its usual termination practices. Thus, if you represent the employee in such a case you might make practice and policy inquiries to ascertain the employer's usual disciplinary procedures.

Ascertaining whether practices comply with industry standards. You may also decide to make practice and policy inquiries when you hope to argue that an opposing party's practice or policy conflicts with an industry standard. For example, assume that you've sued a municipality under the federal Clean Water Act, claiming that the municipality's practices for maintaining catch basins conflict with industry-wide "best management practices." You might depose a municipal official concerning the municipality's catch basin practices.

Ascertaining whether practices comply with legal standards. Another purpose of practice and policy inquiries is to support a claim that an entity's practices violate a normative legal standard. For example, if you claim that a prison's procedures for allowing prisoners to have access to legal materials violates due process, you might depose a prison official concerning those procedures.

Identifying witnesses and documents. Still another purpose of practice and policy inquiries is to identify potential written and electronic materials and witnesses. For instance, if you claim that a company's product was defectively designed, you might depose a company agent concerning the company's normal "R and D" practices. The information can help you identify the departments and employees who may have been involved in designing the product and materials that may have been generated during the design process.

3. WHOM TO DEPOSE

Especially in large organizations, knowledge of policies and practices tends to differ according to a representative's stature in the hierarchy. For example, an upper echelon employee may be quite familiar with an organization's policies, yet have much less familiarity with its actual practices and still less knowledge of the events involved in a specific case. Therefore, whom you choose to depose concerning practices and policies may depend on the argument you are attempting to support.

For example, assume that one of your principal arguments is that your client should prevail because an organization failed to follow its own practices and policies in your client's specific case. Your argument may be that although a company's policies and practices called for employees to be given an opportunity to correct deficiencies in performance before being terminated, your client was given no such opportunity. In such a situation, you may want to depose an upper echelon employee concerning the company's practices and policies. Since the upper echelon employee may have little information about the events involved in your specific case, the employee may be unable to conveniently "match" testimony to your client's experience. The conflicts that may result between what is supposed to happen or generally happens and what happened in your client's case may bolster your argument.

On the other hand, assume one of your arguments on a client's behalf is that both an organization's general practices and what happened to the client conflict with the organization's policies. Here, you may want to depose a lower echelon employee concerning the organization's practices. The lower echelon employee may be less inclined to match usual practices to those called for by an organization's policies.

4. QUESTIONING STRATEGIES REGARDING PRACTICES

To obtain a full description of an organization's practices, you'll typically seek to obtain a chronology or "timeline" of the steps and an account of what happens at each step.[3] The subsections below examine strategies for confronting issues that often arise when deponents testify concerning an organization's practices.

A. RESPONDING TO "IT DEPENDS" ANSWERS

Often, practices are dependent on one or more variables. Consequently, asked a question such as "what then happens," deponents may well answer, "It depends." An effective response is to identify the important and common variables that may alter the practice and then pursue the effects of each.

For example, assume that you have filed a lawsuit against a private company responsible for monitoring detainees being held at an Immigration and Naturalization Service (INS) holding facility. Your complaint alleges that the company's current procedure denies detainees due process. You are taking a "practice and policy" deposition of a security officer for the company, and want to put on the record the company's version of the current procedure that INS detainees generally have to follow to obtain access to legal materials. Your questioning about the procedure proceeds as follows:

---

[3] See Chapter 5.

1. Q: After a detainee asks a unit officer to use a computer in the library, what happens next?

2. A: It depends.

3. Q: Tell me all the things it depends upon.

4. A: It depends on whether the request is made on a weekday or weekend.

5. Q: Does what happens after a detainee asks a unit officer to use a computer in the library depend upon anything else beside whether the request is made on a weekend or a weekday?

6. A: Yes, whether the request is made before or after noon.

7. Q: Does what happens after a detainee asks a unit officer to use the library, depend upon anything else beside whether the request is made on a weekend or a weekday and whether it is made before or after noon?

8. A: No.

Here, the questioning thus far establishes that the procedure depends on the day of the week and the time of day that a request is made. You may now follow up by trying to uncover the reasons for the existence of these variables.

9. Q: All right. Why does the day of the week make a difference?

10. A: Because if the request is made on a Saturday or Sunday, the request will not be processed until Monday. We don't have a library

officer who can do unit pick-ups on the weekends.

11. Q: Any other reason the request can't be processed until Monday?

12. A: No.

[Inquiries about why there is no library officer on weekends omitted]

17. Q: Why does whether the request is made before noon make a difference?

18. A: Because. . .

19. Q: Any other reason?

20. A: No.

At this point, you may probe the effect of each important variable on an entity's practices. For example:

21. Q: Okay. Let's assume that on a weekday and before noon, a detainee asks a unit officer to use the library. What happens next?

22. A: The unit officer would. . .

B. INQUIRE ABOUT EXCEPTIONS

After a deponent has described a practice or policy, you may want to inquire into instances known to the deponent in which the practice was not followed. Such inquiries are likely to be particularly important if your client's claim rests on an individual's or entity's failure to follow usual practices.

Inquiries concerning exceptions might concern both: (1) specific instances in which a general practice was not followed, and (2) broad categories of cases in which a general practice was not followed. When making these inquiries you may ask about both occasions with which a deponent is personally familiar as well as those that a deponent is aware of from the verbal, written or electronic comments of others. The following examples illustrate each of these inquiries.

Inquiring into Specific Instances

1. Q: Ms. Foreman, you've told me about the procedure that the company generally follows when warning employees that their performance has been deemed unsatisfactory. Do you know of any particular instances within the last five years in which this procedure was not followed?

2. A: Yes.

3. Q: As far as you know, on how many occasions was this procedure not followed?

4. A: I can recall two in that period of time.

5. Q: Can you tell me about the first instance?

[Inquiry into each instance omitted]

14. Q: In addition to the two instances you've just told me about, have you heard of any other instances within the last five years in which the usual warning procedure was not followed?

15. A: No.

16. Q: In addition to the two instances you've just told me about, have you read of any other instances in which the usual warning procedure was not followed?

17. A: . . .

Inquiring into Categories of Cases

1. Q: Ms. Foreman, you've told me about the procedure that the company generally uses when warning employees that their performance has been deemed unsatisfactory. Were there any categories of cases within the last five years where this procedure was not used?

2. A: Yes.

3. Q: In what kinds of cases did the company not use the warning procedure you just described?

4. A: Where physical violence was involved.

5. Q: Any other type of case?

6. A: Not that I know of.

7. Q: Have you heard of any other types of cases in which the usual warning procedure was not followed other than in cases involving violence?

8. A: No.

9. Q: Have you read of any other types of cases in which the usual warning procedure was not followed other than in cases involving violence?

10. A. No.

11. Q: Okay, let's return to situations involving physical violence. What. . .

Once you have identified situations in which a common practice was not followed, your follow up questions may focus on why a different practice was followed in those situations, and what that different practice entailed.

C. INQUIRE ABOUT PRIOR AND SUBSEQUENT CHANGES

Both for reasons of relevance and efficiency, inquiries into practices and procedures typically focus on particular time periods. For instance, a practice and policy deposition in a products liability case may emphasize the time period when the allegedly defective product was designed and developed. Similarly, a practice and policy deposition in a case in which you claim that a prison's library practices violate due process is likely to emphasize the practices in effect at the time your clients sought access to prison library materials.

However, evidence tracing prior or subsequent changes to a practice can support a variety of arguments. For example, evidence that an entity changed its practices several times in a relatively short span of time may support an argument that the practices are in such disarray that your adversary's account of current practices is unreliable. Similarly, in a products liability case, evidence that a company changed its design procedures subsequent to the time that it developed an allegedly defective product may support an argument that the company was aware that the prior process did not meet industry standards or may rebut an argument that alternative design procedures were not feasible.

Inquiries such as those below can help you elicit evidence of changes in an adversary's general practices. With respect to each change, you may ask:

- What was the change?
- When was the change made?
- Why was the change made?
- Who made the decision to make the change?

D. DISTINGUISH BETWEEN THE ENTITY'S PRACTICE AND THAT OF THE DEPONENT

When deposing the agent of an organization, you want to distinguish between an organization's practice and the practice followed by the deponent. You can do so by not using "you" when asking about an organization's practice. Instead, ask questions such as "What is the next step the in the **company's** procedure for evaluating an employee?"

Of course, you often want to inquire into both the company's general practice, what the deponent generally does and, if applicable, what the deponent actually did in your case. But you want to keep these lines of inquiry separate.

5. QUESTIONING STRATEGIES REGARDING POLICIES

Whereas "practice" inquiries focus on how organizations typically proceed when taking particular types of actions, "policy" inquiries center on rules or customs that set forth how organizations are **supposed** to operate in given situations. For example, a company may have written or unwritten policies regarding when employees may take "sick leave" and what steps supervisors should follow when disciplining employees.

When questioning a deponent about a **written policy**, you may begin by showing the policy to the deponent and asking the deponent to confirm that the policy was in effect at the relevant time. This strategy tends to encourage a deponent to agree that the policy was the one that was in effect at that time. Alternatively, you may question a deponent as to what policy was in effect at the relevant time without first showing the written policy to the deponent. This strategy may be advantageous if you hope to establish that the policy actually in effect was different from that set forth in written form.

<u>Examples</u>

<u>Beginning policy questioning with a written document</u>: "Please look at item number 6 in Exhibit 3, entitled "Maintaining a Productive Work Environment," and tell me whether during the time that my client was employed by Castiron Co., this exhibit accurately states the company's policy regarding employees' use of

> sick leave to care for family members who are ill."

> Beginning policy questioning without using a written document: "During the time that my client was employed by Castiron Co., what was the company's policy regarding employees' use of sick leave to care for family members who are ill?

Once a deponent testifies to a policy's existence, your follow-up questions, of course, depend on the disputes in a specific case. However, in general the topics are likely to be very similar to those that apply when you make practice-focused inquiries. Thus, in flushing out a written policy you might pursue topics such as the following:

> Is the policy reflected in an online personnel manual?

> Who has copies of the document?

> To what personnel, if any, was the document distributed?

> Who established the policy?

> Do you know of specific situations in which this policy was not applied?

> Do you know of any categories of cases to which this policy was not applied?

> Had the policy been the same during the preceding ___ years?

> If "no," when and why was the policy changed, and who changed the policy?
>
> Has the policy subsequently been changed?
>
> If "yes," when and why was the policy changed, and who changed the policy?

If a deponent is personally unaware of policies concerning a particular subject, you may nonetheless pursue hearsay information. You might ask questions such as:

> Have you ever had discussions with anyone in the organization regarding a policy about _______?
>
> Have you ever heard of any discussions regarding a policy about _______?
>
> Have you seen any documents which refer to a policy about _______?

If a deponent testifies that an organization does not have a written policy with respect to a particular matter, you may then inquire about the possibility of **informal or unwritten policies**. For example, an organization may have an unwritten policy that employees who have been disciplined are ineligible for overtime work assignments for six months. Thus, you might ask a deponent whether the organization has an unwritten policy with respect to a particular subject. If the deponent testifies that such a policy exists, you would then pursue many of the topics suggested above. In addition, you might pursue such topics as whether a written policy on that subject had ever existed, and if not, why not.

6. INQUIRING ABOUT DISCREPANCIES BETWEEN PRACTICES AND POLICIES

Inquiries about practices and policies may reveal that an organization's practices do not match its policies. For instance, you may discover that while a governmental agency's policy provides for a formal hearing for every permit application for discharges of waste into streams, the agency's actual practice does not always include hearings. However, before arguing that a conflict supports a helpful argument, inquire into any reasons or justifications for the conflict. Doing so can help you determine whether your adversary is likely to be able to successfully undermine your argument.

7. INQUIRING ABOUT DISCREPANCIES BETWEEN PRACTICES & POLICIES AND WHAT HAPPENED IN YOUR CLIENT'S CASE

When you discover that there are discrepancies between a practice or policy and what happened in your client's case, you also typically want to inquire into all the potential justifications or reasons for the discrepancies. Once again, you'll want to consider whether the justifications undermine arguments you plan to make.

CHAPTER 15

DEPOSING EXPERTS

To acknowledge the obvious, experts are ubiquitous in civil litigation. Evidence rules have generally widened the scope of acceptable expert testimony, experts have developed increasingly narrow specialties and lawyers have become more creative in using experts to transmit opinions to judges and jurors. Under the Federal Rules of Civil Procedure, parties have a right to depose experts who are likely to testify at trial. Therefore, deposing experts is usually a crucial pretrial activity.

While testifying experts' opinions are generally discoverable, conversations between counsel and expert may or may not be protected from discovery. Most communications between counsel and expert are generally protected as work product and cannot be inquired into by opposing counsel.[1] However, communications relating to the expert's compensation, communications identifying facts or data provided by the attorney upon which the expert relied, and communications relating to assumptions made by the attorney and relied upon by the expert are all discoverable. Moreover, communications that include non-attorneys, such as other experts, may also be subject to discovery.

The bulk of this Chapter describes questioning strategies for deposing designated adverse experts,

---

[1] In some state courts, however, communications between counsel and testifying experts (and draft reports prepared by testifying experts) may be discoverable.

i.e., experts retained by an adverse party to testify at trial. These questioning strategies apply no matter what a particular adverse expert's field of expertise.

The Chapter concludes with a brief discussion of considerations that arise when you depose a percipient expert, e.g., an emergency room physician who treated a plaintiff but has not been retained as an expert witness.

1. MANDATORY DISCLOSURES

When you anticipate offering expert testimony at trial you must make disclosures concerning that testimony. That is, you must voluntarily provide a report to adverse parties which discloses the following with respect to each expert who you retain or specifically employ to provide testimony at trial:

- an expert's opinions;
- the bases and reasons for those opinions;
- information considered by the expert in arriving at the opinions;
- any exhibits that will be used at trial to summarize or support the opinions;
- the expert's qualifications and publications authored within the previous ten years;
- the amount of the expert's compensation; and
- a list of other cases in which the expert has testified (either in a deposition or at trial) during the preceding four years.

Thus, at the time you're preparing to depose experts, you'll likely be able to anticipate much of their testimony.

Your preparation is also likely to be aided by your own experts, whose specialized knowledge you will often rely on to undermine the opinions of adverse experts. If you are unfortunate enough not to have the services of your own expert, you will greatly benefit from thoroughly researching the area of expertise of the adverse expert prior to the deposition. The more you know about the adverse expert's area of expertise, the better you will be able to identify areas of inquiry that might help to undermine the adverse expert's opinions.

2. BEGINNING ADVERSE EXPERT DEPOSITIONS

A. GIVE ADMONITIONS

Even if an expert has participated in more depositions than you, it makes sense to begin the expert's deposition with the same admonitions you would give to any other witness. These admonitions, discussed in Chapter 4, tend to discourage adverse witnesses, whether or not they are experts, from changing their testimony later in a case. The reason is that admonitions allow you to undermine explanations that witnesses commonly give to justify changed testimony.

You may want to supplement the admonitions you give to a lay witness with a few questions that may prevent an expert from giving opinions at trial that were not given in the deposition. You might, for example, ask questions such as the following:

Q: Are you willing and able to state all the opinions at this deposition that you believe you will express at trial?

Q: Do you realize that you may be prevented from giving an opinion at trial if you do not disclose it at this deposition?

Such testimony may help you to convince a judge to prohibit an expert from giving an opinion at trial that is not provided to you at the deposition.

B. CONFIRM THAT YOU HAVE ALL RELEVANT MATERIALS

Reports that you receive usually include or at least refer to the principal materials that adverse experts relied on in forming their opinions. At deposition you want to confirm that you have been provided with copies of or access to all materials an expert reviewed, considered or prepared. For example, indicate to an expert the materials you have been provided with and then ask questions such as:

Q: Have you considered any materials in any form, including digital materials, in connection with this case other than the ones I just mentioned?

Q: Did you generate any materials in any form in connection with this case other than the ones I just mentioned?

Q: Did you generate any interim or draft reports in this case?

Having access to all the materials an adverse expert reviewed, considered or prepared helps to inform your questioning throughout the deposition.

C. ELICIT BACKGROUND INFORMATION

Since a specialized background is what enables experts to offer opinions, background questioning of experts may be extensive. For example, you are likely to probe an expert's background thoroughly when you anticipate asking a judge to exclude an opinion as unreliable.[2] Moreover, careful parsing of an expert's background may promote credibility arguments based on your expert's having more impressive qualifications and experience than your adversary's.

Topics that are often useful to pursue during background questioning include:

- An expert's education and professional training, including both academia (undergraduate, graduate and post-graduate education) and professional or on-the-job training.
- An expert's work experience, including when relevant such matters as work in private industry, government-sponsored research,

---

2 Arguments that expert opinions are unreliable may be based on a witness' personal lack of qualifications, or the unreliability of an expert's methodology. In some states, you might also challenge an opinion because the underlying methodology has not been generally accepted by a relevant field of experts.

teaching (whether in academia or elsewhere), and reasons for changing jobs.

- Awards or honors received and publications authored.
- Organizational affiliations, such as service on the boards of professional organizations or private companies, editorial services for peer-reviewed publications.
- Previous experience as an expert witness, including number and types of cases, interests an expert has represented, opinions an expert has given, and the number of times an expert has qualified as such in court.

Credibility arguments that you might make as a result of such questioning include:

- An adverse expert is a generalist (e.g., a real estate appraiser) testifying to subject matter in a field in which some experts are specialists (e.g., an appraiser of industrial real estate).
- An adverse expert has academic qualifications, but lacks practical experience. For example, in a legal malpractice case a legal academic may qualify to deliver an opinion about whether a situation amounted to a conflict of interest such that an attorney should have advised a client to seek alternate legal counsel. However, the fact that the academic has never practiced law may cause a factfinder to question the academic's credibility.

- An adverse expert's training and practical experience is not a precise "fit" with the facts of a given case. For example, an adverse expert appraiser's experience is in commercial real estate in County A, whereas the property involved in your lawsuit is industrial real estate in County B.
- An adverse expert consistently testifies to similar opinions, suggesting that the expert conforms the facts to pre-existing biases.

3. ELICIT A CHRONOLOGY OF CASE-RELATED ACTIVITIES

Generally, the meat of expert depositions consists of eliciting and challenging opinions. Before doing so, it's generally a good idea to first elicit a detailed chronology of an expert's case-related activities. An expert's chronology consists of the significant case-related activities from the date of first contact by opposing counsel to the date of deposition.[3] Obtaining such a chronology promotes thoroughness and helps you understand and later probe the bases of an expert's opinions. For example, by eliciting a chronology you generally:

- Learn when the expert agreed to serve and what the expert was aware of at that time. If an expert agreed to serve before reviewing pertinent information, you may argue that the

---

[3] Chapter 5 describes useful questioning strategies for obtaining a chronology.

expert's evaluation and opinion is less than objective.

- Learn what non-privileged information opposing counsel provided to the expert, and when it was provided. If your adversary has given an expert incomplete information, or if the information was delayed, you may argue that the expert's conclusions are based on a distorted picture of the evidence. Uncovering the substance of opposing counsel's discussions with an expert, particularly during deposition preparation sessions, may reveal information about counsel's view of the strengths and weaknesses of a case.

- Develop a picture early on of what an expert did to arrive at her opinions. For example, what methodology did an expert use? What tests did the expert conduct or fail to conduct? What research did the expert conduct or fail to conduct? What interim reports or documents did the expert create or receive, and what witnesses did the expert speak with and when?

- Identify assistants or independent third parties and their contributions to an expert's investigation. This information helps you decide if you need additional depositions.

- Identify exhibits the expert has prepared for use at trial, and find out when the exhibits were prepared and what information the expert had at the time they were prepared.

- Learn what the expert did to prepare for the deposition. To whom did he talk? Did he talk to opposing counsel? Were non-privileged matters discussed? If so, what was said?

When you conclude a chronology, you might also ask whether an expert anticipates extending an investigation beyond the date of deposition. If so, you might follow up by asking what the expert intends to do and why the expert needs to do it. You can then attack credibility if the expert neglects to follow through. Alternatively, if the expert does intend to conduct further investigation, you may want to postpone the conclusion of the deposition until after the investigation is complete.[4]

One approach to eliciting a chronology is to elicit details as the chronology emerges. For instance, if the first event in a chronology is a "January 26 phone call," you might find out as much as you can about the call before finding out what happened next.

Alternatively, and especially when a chronology is likely to be lengthy, you may want to obtain a brief overview of activities before exploring any of them in depth. An overview often helps you make judgments about which events are most important, thus promoting efficiency. The following example suggests how you might elicit a chronological overview. Assume that you are deposing Lex Purt, an engineer

---

[4] To do so, do not adjourn the deposition when you have finished questioning. Instead, try to have opposing counsel agree to continue the deposition at a date when the expert will have completed her work. This saves you the trouble of trying to notice a second deposition, for which you usually need court permission.

retained by the defendant in a product liability case involving the alleged substandard design of a bicycle helmet. Overview questioning might go as follows:

1. Q: What's the first time that you heard about this case?

2. A: It was on January 10, when I got an email from Jean, the defense attorney. Jean's message provided basic background information and asked if I'd be willing to evaluate the case for the purpose of providing expert testimony. I agreed to do so, and she said that she'd send a file folder to me.

3. Q: Then what happened?

4. A: I texted Jean a couple of days later. I'd read the file, and I told her I'd be willing to look into what happened and give her an opinion, and that I'd be available to testify if my evaluation of the evidence supported her client's claims.

5. Q: What's the next thing you can recall happening in connection with this case?

6. A: I'd asked Jean to send over transcripts of depositions that had previously been taken, and I read through those. Around the same time, I looked through a treatise, "Bicycle Helmet Design in a Nutshell" and talked with Jack Aranda, who I believe at the time was the President of the National Association of Bicycle Helmet Manufacturers.

7. Q: What time period are we talking about when you're reviewing transcripts and the treatise and talking to Mr. Aranda?

8. A: Probably late January. Jean had told me that the case was on a fast track and that I needed to gather information quickly.

9. Q: Okay, what happened next that is in any way related to this case?

10. A: I toured the defendant's factory. I talked to various employees, particularly in the quality control department, and received password access to files containing design specifications and other records.

11. Q: Between the time you reviewed the transcripts and before you toured the factory, did anything else happen related to this case?

12. A: Well, I talked to Jean to set up the tour of the factory.

13. Q: Now, after touring the factory, what happened next?

14. A: . . .

4. ELICIT ALL OPINIONS

The voluntary disclosures required by FRCP 26(a)(2)(B) should set forth all the opinions to which an expert will testify at trial.[5] A chronology of an expert's activities also typically surfaces the opinions

---

[5] An opinion that the party failed to disclose may be excluded by pretrial motion.

that an expert will give at trial. Nevertheless, before beginning to probe each opinion, it makes sense to ask experts whether they have any opinions that they have not yet mentioned. For example:

1. Q: Ms. Jetson, showing you what has been marked as Exhibit 23, this is the report you prepared in this case, correct?

2. A. Yes.

3. Q: In Exhibit 23, you state that it is your opinion that my client's car was traveling at a speed of about 65 m.p.h. when it struck the bridge abutment, correct?

4. A: Yes.

5. Q: Do you have any opinions in any way related to this case in addition to the opinion that my client's car was traveling at a speed of 65 m.p.h. when it struck the bridge abutment?

6. A: No.

7. Q: So you do not have any opinion about whether or not my client lost control of the car before striking the abutment, do you?

8. A: No, I was not asked to give an opinion on that.

9. Q: And you do not have any opinion about whether or not my client was driving negligently on the day of the accident, correct?

10. A: That is correct.

11. Q: And you do not have any opinion about what caused my client's car to strike the abutment, correct?

12. A: That's right. My only opinion relates to the speed of the car at impact.

In this example, Nos. 1–6 establish that the expert has only one opinion in the case. You could have concluded your question with question No 6. However, testimony such as in Nos. 7–12 provide added assurance that an expert will not provide additional opinions at trial. If the expert did try to provide additional opinions at trial, Nos. 7–12 help you to convince a judge to exclude them.

5. ELICIT THE BASIS FOR EACH OPINION

When an expert provides an opinion, the expert typically reaches that opinion by evaluating case-specific evidence or factual information in light of one or more premises drawn from an expert's specialized knowledge. For example, a medical expert's opinion that injuries to a child were intentionally inflicted may be based in part on case specific evidence of x-rays showing that the child's leg had a spiral fracture, and the expert's specialized knowledge that validates the premise that such a spiral fracture generally results from an intentional twisting of the leg.

For each opinion, you typically want to obtain both the evidentiary basis and the relevant specialized knowledge relied on by the expert.

A. ELICIT THE EVIDENTIARY BASIS FOR EACH OPINION

To obtain the evidentiary basis for an opinion, you can simply ask the expert for all the evidence supporting an opinion. Experts can rely on many different types of information as the evidentiary basis for an opinion. For example, the evidentiary or factual basis for an expert's opinion may include:

- Tangible evidence, e.g., a blood sample, a fingerprint or a hair sample.
- Information obtained by the expert from reviewing written discovery, witness statements, deposition transcripts, and other materials.
- Information generated directly by the expert, e.g., test results or the results of interviews or other activities conducted directly by the expert.
- Factual assumptions made by the expert at the direction of the retaining party, e.g., an expert calculating damages in a wrongful termination case may have been told to assume that the plaintiff would have worked at the company until the age of 60 if she had not been discharged.

B. ELICIT THE SPECIALIZED KNOWLEDGE UNDERLYING EACH OPINION

The background factors that qualify experts to render opinions include knowledge, skill, experience, training or education. This specialized knowledge usually falls into one or all of the following categories:

- Experience
- Training and education
- Authorities (e.g., treatises, research studies, industry standards, etc.)

For each opinion rendered by an expert you will typically want to obtain the specialized knowledge that the expert relies upon to reach that opinion. For example, return to the case of the medical expert who opined that injuries to a child were intentionally inflicted based on x-rays showing that the child's leg had a spiral fracture. To obtain the expert's specialized knowledge supporting this opinion you might ask questions such as the following:

- Tell me all the reasons you believe a spiral fracture indicates that the fracture was the result of an intentional injury.
- What training do you have that supports your opinion that a spiral fracture indicates an intentional injury?
- Is there anything in your educational background that you rely on to support your opinion that a spiral fracture indicates an intentional injury?
- What medical authorities support your opinion that a spiral fracture indicates an intentional injury?

6. UNDERMINING AN EXPERT OPINION

You can typically undermine an adverse expert's opinion by challenging one or both of the following:

(1) The accuracy or sufficiency of the evidentiary basis for the opinion.

(2) The adequacy of the specialized knowledge of the expert.

The remainder of the Chapter examines a variety of questioning strategies for challenging adverse experts' opinions on one or both of these grounds. Typically, the strategies you pursue in any individual case depend on factual disputes in the case and the areas of disagreement between an adverse expert's opinions and the conflicting opinions of your own expert. Your own expert will often be able to suggest which of the strategies discussed below are most likely to be effective and may even be able to suggest specific lines of inquiry. You may use one or more of these strategies with respect to each opinion of an adverse expert.

7. CHALLENGE #1—AN EXPERT'S SPECIALIZED KNOWLEDGE IS INADEQUATE

You may undermine an opinion by probing the adequacy of an expert's specialized knowledge. Here, your questions are likely to concentrate on the three topics that typically serve as the sources of specialized knowledge: experience, training and education, and authorities.

For an illustration of how you might probe an expert's specialized knowledge, assume that you represent the defendant manufacturer of an automobile tire that ruptured and caused a serious accident. You are deposing the plaintiff's expert, who has opined in a report provided to you that a manufacturing defect caused the tire to fail, and there was no misuse of the tire by the plaintiff. You contend that the rupture was caused by misuse of the tire. To attempt to undermine the adequacy of the expert's specialized knowledge, you might proceed as follows:

1. Q: What is your opinion as to why the tire failed?

2. A: A manufacturing defect caused the tire to rupture.

3. Q: What is there about the tire that leads you to conclude that there was a manufacturing defect?

4. A: My inspection of the tire indicated that the tread had separated from the tire's inner steel belt. When that happens, if the separation isn't the result of misuse, such as under-inflating the tire, then the separation must be due to a defect in the way the tire was made or designed. In my opinion, this separation was not the result of misuse.

5. Q: Let's first address your opinion that the separation was not caused by misuse. What evidence supports your opinion that the tire was not misused?

6. A: When a tire is misused, I'd expect to find physical symptoms consistent with misuse. These symptoms are greater tread wear on the shoulder than on the center of the tire, bead grooves on the inside of a tire's rim, deteriorated side walls, and marks on a tire's rim flange. Unless I find at least two of these symptoms, I conclude that there was no misuse. I didn't find two of those symptoms in this case.

7. Q: Is there any other evidence that supports your opinion that the tire was not misused?

8. A: No. Not in this case.

9. Q: What experience do you have that allows you to say that there is no misuse unless at least two of these symptoms are present?

10. A: I have an engineering degree and I worked for Goodstone tire company for 15 years, specializing in tire failure analysis.

11. Q: What other experience do you have that allows you to say that there is no misuse unless at least two of these symptoms are present?

12. A: I don't have any other such experience.

13. Q: We'll talk about your work at Goodstone a little later. Right now, I'd like to know how many ruptured tires have you examined to try to determine whether at least two of these symptoms are necessary to conclude that the tire was misused?

14. A: I've only done that three times, when I have been asked to testify as an expert in litigation.

15. Q: How many of these cases involved the same make of tire as the one involved in this case?

16. A: None.

(Additional questions about these three cases are omitted).

17. Q: Now, have you received any training where you were told that there is no misuse unless at least two of these symptoms are present on a tire?

18. A: No. Not specifically. But my approach is based on my experience and my education and training as an engineer.

19. Q: Are you aware of any research reports, articles, opinions by other experts or any other authorities that support your opinion that there is no misuse unless at least two of these symptoms are present?

20. A: No. I developed this methodology on my own. . .

Arguments that you might be able to make after probing these three specialized knowledge factors include:

- An opinion is entitled to little weight because an expert's education and training took place many years ago.

- An opinion is entitled to little weight because an expert's experience relates to situations different from those involved in your case.
- An opinion is entitled to little weight because an expert's methodology is not generally accepted in the scientific community.
- An opinion is entitled to little weight (or is inadmissible) because an expert's knowledge is based on unreliable methodology.

8. CHALLENGE #2—"EXCEPTIONS" DETRACT FROM AN OPINION'S ACCURACY

As noted above, expert opinions rest on one or more premises. And such premises are often true less than 100% of the time. For example, based on the premise that spiral fractures in young children are generally the result of an intentional injury, a medical expert might testify to an opinion that a child with a spiral fracture was a child abuse victim. Similarly, based on a premise that speakers usually make unique speech sounds, a linguistics expert might testify that a comparison of two voices indicates that both are the voice of the same person. Because the premises relied on by experts are typically not true 100% of the time, almost all expert opinions are subject to "exceptions." Depositions give you an opportunity to probe for such "exceptions." Consider the following example.

Assume that you represent an oil company that owns an oil tanker that ran aground and caused property damage and a variety of environmental harms. Your adversary claims that the tanker ran aground because the captain was drunk and therefore unable to recognize that the tanker was off course. The deponent is Dr. Peter Laddy, a voice identification expert. Based on his analysis of the captain's voice recorded by the ship's audio tapes before and after the ship ran aground, Dr. Laddy arrived at the opinion that the captain was under the influence of alcohol at the time that the ship ran aground. Dr. Laddy's factual support for this conclusion is that the captain's voice was deeper and huskier, and the captain spoke more slowly, around the time of the grounding than before and after the grounding. Your search for exceptions might proceed as follows:

1. Q: Dr. Laddy, is it fair to say that your opinion is that as a general rule, evidence that a speaker's voice was deeper and huskier than normal indicates that the speaker was under the influence of alcohol?

2. A: Yes.

3. Q: Are there factors other than the consumption of alcohol that might cause a person's voice to become deeper and huskier than usual?

4. A: Yes. Many drugs that would have that effect.

5. Q: Are there factors other than drugs that might make a person's speech deeper and huskier than normal?

6. A: Yes. There have been some research findings that the speech sounds of people who talk under conditions of stress are deeper and huskier than normal. A study by Dr. Allenson is perhaps the best-known research in this area. However, this has never been a consistent finding—most of the studies indicate that the speech patterns of subjects are unaffected by stress.

7. Q: Nevertheless, some research indicates that speech patterns may sometimes be affected by stress?

8. A: Yes.

9. Q: And that effect is to make a person's voice huskier and deeper than normal?

10. A: Yes.

11. Q: Are there any factors, other than drugs and stress, that might make a person's speech deeper and huskier than normal?

12. A: Well, someone can consciously speak in a deeper and huskier manner.

13. Q: Are there any factors, other than drugs, stress and a conscious attempt to alter one's voice that that might make a person's speech deeper and huskier than normal?

14. A: I don't think so, no.

15. Q: Well, when a person speaks within a minute after being awakened, might that have a

tendency to make the person's voice deeper and huskier than normal?

16. A: That would be a possibility, yes.

17. Q: Recording C was made minutes before the ship ran aground, correct?

18. A: That's correct.

19. Q: I want you to assume that at the time Recording C was made the captain was under stress and had just been awakened a couple of minutes before the recording was made. Would those assumptions make you less confident in your opinion that the captain was under the influence of alcohol at the time that the recording was made?

20. A: Not really.

21. Q: Why not?

22. A: Because my opinion is also based on the fact that the captain's voice was slower than normal, that is, that he spoke more slowly on Recording C than he did on recordings A or B.

23. Q: Let's talk about that. Dr. Laddy, is it fair to say that it is your opinion that as a general rule, someone's talking more slowly than normal is evidence that the speaker is under the influence of alcohol?

24. A: Yes.

25. Q: Are there things, other than the consumption of alcohol, that might make a person's speech slower than normal?

26. A: Yes. . .

Here, the expert's opinion rests on the premise that deeper, huskier and unusually slow speech tends to prove that a speaker has consumed alcohol. (Nos. 1–2; 23–24). Instead of trying to directly challenge the validity of this premise, you have identified exceptions to the premise that when a speaker's voice is deeper and huskier it tends to show that a speaker has consumed alcohol. (Nos. 3–16). And you have begun to search for exceptions for the premise involving unusually slow speech. (Nos. 25–26). If you can show that the facts supporting an exception are likely to be present, you can undermine the expert's opinion.

9. CHALLENGE #3—CONFLICTING AUTHORITIES UNDERMINE AN OPINION

Probes for exceptions generally assume the validity of a premise underlying an expert's opinion. Another type of challenge is to attack directly the validity of underlying premises. Typically, this type of challenge involves searching for or confronting an expert with authorities (e.g., treatises, research studies, industry standards etc.) that conflict with the premises on which the expert relies.

For example, assume that a medical expert has testified to an opinion that a fracture of a three-year-old child's arm was intentionally inflicted. The expert's opinion relies heavily on x-rays showing that the child had a spiral fracture. Questioning about contrary authorities might proceed as follows:

1. Q: Dr. Weil, you testified that the fact that the child had a spiral fracture of the humerus bone supports your opinion that the fracture was the result of an intentional injury, correct?

2. A: That's correct.

3. Q: Are you aware of any authorities that conclude that spiral fractures to the humerus bones of young children generally do not indicate intentional injury, but rather are consistent with accidental injury?

4. A: Yes. There have been two studies recently reported in medical journals saying that.

5. Q: Other than these two studies, are you aware of any other authorities that conclude that spiral fractures to the humerus bones of young children generally do not indicate intentional injury, but rather are consistent with accidental injury?

6. A: No.

7. Q: Given these two recent studies that you mentioned, why do you say that the spiral fracture tends to support your opinion that the injury in this case was intentional?

8. A: I think both of those studies were seriously flawed.

9. Q: Please tell me all the ways in which you think these studies were flawed.

10. A: Well. . .

Note that after uncovering a conflicting authority, you ask the expert why he nevertheless maintains his opinion. If the expert has a reasonable explanation, better that you learn it sooner than later.

10. CHALLENGE #4—AN OPINION IS BASED ON INACCURATE INFORMATION FROM THIRD PARTIES ("GARBAGE IN, GARBAGE OUT")

As discussed above, the evidentiary basis for an expert's opinion may be information gleaned from such third-party sources as discovery responses, witness statements, deposition transcripts or other materials. At deposition, one way to challenge an opinion is to establish that an expert has assumed the accuracy of such information. You may be able to challenge the opinion by later showing that the information is not accurate.

Example

You represent Pat, one of a group of police officers who has been sued by an arrestee, Mr. Kang, for allegedly using excessive force during Kang's arrest. You are deposing Kang's expert, who earlier testified to an opinion that the force was excessive, in part because Pat should not have kicked Kang in the head after Kang was lying on the ground. Pat denies kicking Kang in the head and contends that Kang's head was injured when Kang fell and hit it on a curb. Your questioning proceeds as follows:

1. Q: Your opinion is that Officer Pat used excessive force, in part because he kicked Mr. Kang in the head?

2. A: That's right.

3. Q: Would you tell me all the information you are aware of that indicates that Officer Pat kicked Mr. Kang in the head?

4. A: Mr. Kang testified in his deposition that he was kicked in the head by Pat. And the medical records indicate that Kang had a severe contusion on the right side of his head where he said he was kicked.

5. Q: Is there any other information that you are aware of that indicates that Officer Pat kicked Mr. Kang in the head?

6. A: No, not that I know of.

7. Q: You were not asked to undertake an investigation or an analysis of the facts of this case to determine whether Mr. Kang was telling the truth when he said he was kicked in the head, correct?

8. A: That's true.

9. Q: You are assuming that Mr. Kang is telling the truth about being kicked in the head, correct?

10. A: I suppose that's true, but it seems to me that Mr. Kang's testimony is consistent with the medical records.

11. Q: You have no medical training, correct?

12. A: That's correct.

13. Q: So you don't know whether the medical records are consistent with Mr. Kang having hit his head on a street curb when he fell to the ground as the officers were attempting to arrest him, correct?

14. A: That's true.

15. Q: And you never personally talked to Mr. Kang about what happened on the night of his arrest, correct?

16. A: That's true.

17. Q: Now, if you found out that Officer Pat did not kick Mr. Kang in the head, would that change your opinion about whether the officers used excessive force on the night in question?[6]

18. A: No, because there are other reasons that the force used by the officers was excessive.

19. Q: If you found out that Officer Pat did not kick Mr. Kang in the head, would you be less confident in your opinion about whether the officers used excessive force on the night in question?

---

[6] Evidence rules generally allow you to pose hypothetical questions to experts.

20. A: No, I would not.

21. Q: Why not?

22. A: Because even if Pat did not kick Kang in the head, the officers hit him in the legs with their batons after he was lying on the ground and offering no resistance, and that constitutes excessive force.

23. Q: Would you tell me all the information you are aware of that indicates that when the officers hit Kang in the legs with their batons, he was not offering resistance?

24. A: Well. . .

In this example, you first elicit all the information the expert is aware of that indicates that Pat kicked Kang in the head. (Nos. 3–6). Next, you establish that the expert has no first-hand knowledge of that information's accuracy. (Nos. 7–16).

Note that after establishing the expert's lack of firsthand knowledge, you try to establish that the expert's opinion, or his confidence level in that opinion, would change if the information from the third party proved false. (Nos. 17–22). Such concessions are important if you can produce evidence undermining the accuracy of the information on which an opinion rests. In addition, you might argue that an expert's insistence that an opinion would be unaffected by a drop in evidentiary support is implausible.

11. CHALLENGE #5—UNDERMINE THE RESULTS OF SCIENTIFIC TESTS OR TECHNICAL PROCEDURES

Evidence supporting an expert's opinion may consist of the results of scientific tests or procedures. For example, an expert testifying that your client was under the influence of alcohol at the time of an auto accident may rely on the results of a breathalyzer test. And an expert's opinion that property is contaminated with toxic waste may be based on the results of a soils test.

The topics you inquire into to undermine the results of a test or procedure obviously vary dramatically from case to case. And your own expert's input will be particularly helpful when developing lines of inquiry for this challenge. There are, however, several areas you should at least consider probing to try to undercut the accuracy of test results and procedures:

- **Procedural Irregularities**—Generally, the accuracy of test results hinges on proper procedures. Thus, you can inquire into topics such as whether an expert knows what procedures were followed when a test was given, and if so the propriety of those procedures. For example, before using a breathalyzer to test for the percentage of alcohol in blood, a technician should first conduct an "open room test." This test determines whether chemicals that might interfere with the accuracy of a test are present in the room where a test is given.

Results may therefore be inaccurate if an open room test was not performed.

- **Inherent Uncertainties**—Test results can be inaccurate even if proper procedures are followed. Thus, you can inquire into a test's accuracy. For example, has accuracy been investigated, and if so has an error rate been established? For example, some instruments measure the amount of alcohol in a person's blood by passing infrared light through a breath sample and measuring the amount of infrared light absorbed by the alcohol molecules in the sample. Even when all proper procedures are followed, however, molecules other than alcohol that absorb infrared light may be present in a person's breath. The presence of such molecules in a breath sample therefore tends to produce inaccurate test results.

- **Sample Errors**—Test results are inaccurate when the wrong sample is used or when a sample becomes contaminated before testing by age or by improper storage or handling. In addition, a sample may become contaminated or degraded as a result of prior tests or procedures.

- **Failure to Conduct Additional Tests**—Opinions that rely on test results may be undercut with evidence of an expert's failure to conduct additional, reasonable investigation. For instance, if a medical expert bases an opinion that brain damage is permanent on the results of lab tests and x-rays, you might ask whether other tests, such as a "CAT" scan, were performed. If not, elicit an expert's reasons for not doing so.

- **Reliability of Methodology**—Under the Federal Rules of Evidence as currently interpreted by the U.S. Supreme Court, an expert opinion may be inadmissible at trial if based on evidence resulting from unreliable methodologies or procedures. No single standard of reliability exists. Factors that judges may consider include whether experts' methods have been generally accepted in the community of experts with relevant expertise; whether methods have been published in peer-reviewed journals; and whether methods have been scientifically tested and error rates established. You may want to inquire into such topics at deposition, particularly if an adverse expert's opinions are based on novel or untested methods. The information you develop may lead to arguments concerning both the weight and the admissibility of opinions.

12. CHALLENGE #6—AN INVESTIGATION IS INCOMPLETE OR UNTIMELY

You may be able to show that an expert's investigation was insufficient or incomplete. For example, if an arson expert relies exclusively on burn pattern evidence when concluding that a fire was intentionally set, you might probe to determine whether the expert could have talked to the warehouse manager and the night watchman working on the night of the fire to obtain further relevant information. Or if an engineer testifies that a tire ruptured due to a manufacturing defect, you might probe to determine why the expert only looked at pictures of the ruptured tire rather than examining the tire itself.

You may also be able to undermine an expert opinion by showing that the expert's investigation was untimely. For example, assume that an expert opines as to the cause of a mudslide that damaged a residence. You may be able to show that the expert first visited the site several weeks after the slide first occurred. If so, you can then probe to determine whether the expert knows if the conditions that she observed were the same as the conditions immediately after the slide. If the conditions may have changed, you have undermined the expert's opinion.

13. CHALLENGE #7—AN EXPERT IS BIASED

In theory, experts are neutrals with no stake in lawsuits' outcomes. In practice this may not be accurate. And depositions provide an opportunity to explore topics that might yield grist for an argument that an adverse expert is biased and therefore not credible. Common topics relevant to bias include:

- **An expert's relationships with opposing counsel and parties**. For example, has opposing counsel previously employed an expert? If so, how often and in what cases?

Does an expert have a personal relationship with opposing counsel or the opposing party?

- **The percentage of an expert's time and income devoted to testifying as an expert.** Jurors may distrust "professional witnesses" whose main occupation consists of hiring themselves out as experts.

- **If not included in a required disclosure report, the number and types of cases in which an expert has previously been retained, and by which party (plaintiff or defendant) an expert was retained.** Repeatedly taking the same position (e.g., that doctors were not negligent) suggests that an expert's opinion reflects a pre-existing bias rather than an independent analysis of the evidence in a particular case.

- **An expert's compensation.** To the extent that complete information is not set forth in a disclosure report, you can ask how much an expert has been paid to date, and how much additional compensation an expert expects to receive for post-deposition work, including testifying at trial. Although compensation of experts is routine, overly generous compensation arrangements may suggest that an expert is biased.

- **Prior inconsistent statements.** Ideally, prior to deposition you will be familiar with relevant statements an expert has made in books, articles, prior cases, etc. At deposition, you might confront the expert with conflicts between prior and current statements to determine if the expert has a reasonable explanation for the conflicts.

14. GARNER SUPPORT FOR YOUR EXPERT'S OPINION

In addition to trying to undermine an adverse expert's opinion, you may also question the expert with an eye toward garnering evidence supporting your own expert's opinion(s). You cannot, of course, expect the adverse expert to abandon an opinion in favor of one championed by your expert. But you can often get an adverse expert to acknowledge one or more of the following:

- Evidence relied upon by your expert is accurate (or at least that the adverse expert has no reason to believe it is not accurate).
- Evidence relied upon by your expert is consistent with or supports your expert's opinion.
- Authorities relied upon by your expert are reliable, are generally relied on by others in the field, and have been relied on by the adverse expert in the past.
- The tests conducted by your expert are likely to produce results that are relevant to your expert's opinion, and the methods used to conduct the tests are proper.

- Your expert's experience and training are generally likely to provide someone with the specialized knowledge that is relevant to your expert's opinion.
- Your expert has a good reputation in her field of expertise.

In each of the areas, if an adverse expert will not make the acknowledgement you seek, you might follow up by asking for the basis for any refusal. For example, if an adverse expert will not acknowledge that evidence relied upon by your expert is consistent with or supports your expert's opinion, you might ask for an explanation of why the evidence is not consistent with your expert's opinion. This information helps your expert prepare for deposition or trial.

15. OPPOSING PARTY'S DUTY TO SUPPLEMENT EXPERT'S DEPOSITION TESTIMONY

Opposing parties have an obligation to supplement the answers in their expert witness deposition testimony with information learned after the expert has been deposed. The FRCP imposes no such explicit obligation to supplement deposition testimony of a lay witness with information learned after the deposition is complete.

16. PREPARING YOUR OWN EXPERT FOR DEPOSITION

Communications between counsel and experts are typically protected as work product and may not be inquired into by opposing counsel at deposition. However, communications that involve non-attorneys, such as other experts, or communications relating to compensation, facts, data or assumptions that you provide to the expert are not protected. As a result, you may need to make strategic decisions about how you prepare your expert and think carefully about who is present during the preparation session.

17. DEPOSING PERCIPIENT EXPERTS

This Chapter has focused on strategies and techniques for deposing adverse forensic experts, i.e., experts retained by an adversary for the purpose of giving testimony. Some experts, however, are not retained; they are percipient witnesses. Examples:

- An emergency room physician who treated a plaintiff immediately after an auto accident and will testify to the nature and extent of the injuries.
- A county health inspector who inspected an apartment house and will testify to the extent to which the building complied with building codes.

Unlike retained experts, percipient experts generally are not required to provide voluntary disclosures under FRCP 26(a)(2)(B). However, counsel still must disclose the subject matter on which such expert may testify and a summary of the facts and opinions to which such expert is expected to testify. Thus, you'll often be able to anticipate much of what percipient experts are likely to say at deposition. The following considerations arise when you decide whether to depose percipient experts:

- If a percipient expert's testimony is likely to be damaging, you might elicit the expert's version of significant events, attempt to undermine harmful evidence, and search for helpful testimony. To the extent that a percipient expert provides damaging opinions, you may attempt to challenge them using the strategies described earlier in the Chapter. However, you generally should not search for harmful evidence. Such a search often makes sense when you depose adverse witnesses because opposing counsel usually has the opportunity to develop additional harmful evidence after a deposition concludes. By contrast, opposing counsel is less likely to have access to a percipient expert outside the confines of a deposition. Thus, if you don't bring out harmful evidence at deposition, opposing counsel may never learn of it.

- If a percipient expert's testimony is likely to be helpful, consider whether it makes sense to depose the expert. Typical downsides of taking a deposition in these circumstances are the expense of a deposition and providing your adversary with a venue for undermining the helpful testimony. Moreover, a deposition may be unnecessary because percipient experts typically leave paper or digital trails of their observations, and much of the trail is likely to be admissible in evidence (say, as a business record) even if the expert is unavailable to testify at trial. Especially since these records may be sufficient to support your position at settlement negotiations, you may decide to forgo taking a deposition. On the other hand, if a case justifies the expense, or if an expert's records are of poor quality or are unlikely to be admissible in evidence, you may want to take a deposition to preserve the helpful testimony.

- If you do decide to depose a percipient expert whose testimony is likely to be helpful, elicit the helpful testimony and foundational testimony establishing that the testimony is accurate. To the extent that an expert can testify to helpful opinions based on specialized knowledge, elicit foundational evidence establishing the expert's qualifications to testify as an expert.

A Checklist for Expert Depositions

Below you will find a Checklist that summarizes the various approaches you might pursue when deposing an adverse expert. You might have this Checklist (or a customized version of it) available at a deposition of an adverse expert to remind you of possible topics and questions. Additionally, you can also use the Checklist during deposition preparation.

Checklist for Deposing an Adverse Expert

1. **Beginning the Deposition**
   - Give Admonitions
   - Confirm That You Have All Relevant Materials
   - Obtain Background Information

2. **Elicit a Chronology of Case Related Activities**

3. **Elicit All Opinions**

4. **Elicit the Basis for Each Opinion**
   - Evidentiary Basis
   - Specialized Knowledge—(Experience, Training and Education, Authorities)

5. **Undermine Each Opinion**
   - Challenge #1—Expert's Specialized Knowledge Is Inadequate
   - Challenge #2—"Exceptions" Detract from an Opinion's Accuracy
   - Challenge #3—Conflicting Authorities Undermine an Opinion
   - Challenge #4—Opinion Is Based on Inaccurate Information from Third Parties

- Challenge #5—Undermine the Results of Scientific Tests or Technical Procedures
    - (Procedural Irregularities, Inherent Uncertainties, Sample Errors, Failure to Conduct Additional Tests or Reliability of Methodology)
- Challenge #6—An Investigation Is Incomplete or Untimely
- Challenge #7—An Expert Is Biased
    - (Relationship with Counsel, Income from Testifying as an Expert, Testifying for Only Plaintiffs or Defendants, Prior Inconsistent Statements)

6. **Garner Support for Your Expert's Opinion**

CHAPTER 16

PREPARING DEPONENTS

Pre-deposition meetings with deponents can ease their anxiety and help them respond effectively at deposition. In addition, such meetings may alert you to the need to gather more information and/or documents before a deposition begins. This Chapter focuses on strategies for preparing clients and concludes with a section devoted to preparation of non-clients.

1. PRE-MEETING PREPARATION

The subsections below examine steps that you may take prior to pre-deposition preparation meetings with clients.

A. REVIEW THE VALIDITY OF DOCUMENT REQUESTS

The Notice of Deposition or Subpoena Duces Tecum that requires your client's attendance may request the production of documents. If so, decide whether you intend to object to any portion of the request pursuant to FRCP 34(b) or FRCP 26(b).

B. REVIEW PERTINENT DOCUMENTS

Prior to meeting with clients, gather and review the documents you will produce at the deposition in response to deposing counsel's request as well as any other documents that may be pertinent to a client's testimony. For example, you might want to examine all case-related documents that bear a client's name, documents that may refresh a client's memory, and documents about which a client is likely to be questioned.

C. PREPARE A CASE CHRONOLOGY

If you have not already done so, prepare a case chronology reflecting each party's versions of the significant events in a case. Reviewing relevant portions of a chronology with a client can refresh the client's recollection and help the client testify accurately.[1]

D. HELP IDENTIFY THE PERSON(S) MOST KNOWLEDGEABLE FOR DEPOSITIONS OF ENTITIES

If opposing counsel notices a deposition of an entity (i.e., a corporation, partnership or government entity),[2] you should make a reasonable effort to help your client identify and produce the person(s) most knowledgeable with respect to the subjects listed in the notice. If a client does not currently have a person who is knowledgeable about subjects listed in the notice, inform the client that it has an obligation to take reasonable steps to educate a representative to testify on any such subject.

---

1 If you use a chronology to refresh recollection, you may have to provide it to your adversary. You can, of course, go over the information in the chronology without showing the document to a client and avoid any risk of having to produce it.

2 For a discussion of 30(b)(6) depositions, see Chapter 13.

E. ARRANGE TO MEET THE CLIENT

When it comes to scheduling a client's preparation meeting, your primary considerations include how many meetings may be needed and how far in advance of deposition to meet.

You may need more than one meeting to prepare a client, especially when:

- A case is complex;
- A deposition is likely to be lengthy;
- A client is unsophisticated and nervous;
- Events likely to be asked about are no longer fresh in a client's mind.[3]

On the other hand, a single meeting or even a phone call or online chat may be adequate if a deposition is likely to be short and a client's testimony is straightforward.

Whether or not you hold a single meeting or multiple ones, hold meetings far enough in advance of depositions to allow clients to gather additional information or documents should such actions be necessary.

2. TELL CLIENTS WHAT DOCUMENTS TO REVIEW (AND NOT REVIEW)

Any case-related document that a client reads in preparation for deposition may have to be turned

---

[3] Of course, you must also take into account a client's willingness to spend time and pay fees for the preparation.

over to an adversary—even if the document would otherwise be privileged. Therefore, tell clients what documents they should and should not review when preparing to meet with you.

Clients may also have to disclose the identities of anyone they talk to when preparing for deposition, as well as the content of any such conversations. Consequently, advise clients to whom they may speak concerning case-related subjects.

Advice you may give a client with respect to these matters may go as follows:

> Jenni, between today and the time we meet next Thursday, it will be useful for you to review your correspondence file with Trans Co. relating to this project. Be sure to review carefully the transcripts I sent you of the depositions of George Murray and Nancy Iorillo. However, I don't want you to look over the memo I sent you in February of last year. If you look that over, we may have to turn that memo over to Billings' lawyer and I prefer not to do that. Also, please don't talk to anyone about the case and your deposition between now and the time we meet unless you clear it with me first.

3. CONDUCTING PREPARATION MEETINGS

The subsections below describe matters you are likely to address when you meet to prepare clients for a deposition.

A. EXPLAIN WHAT THE MEETING ENTAILS

Simple, brief explanations of what you plan to do during a preparation meeting can help ease the anxiety of a client who is unfamiliar with the deposition process. Offering clients an opportunity to ask questions can surface concerns you would not have anticipated. Alleviating clients' concerns early on helps clients pay attention to your inquiries rather than dwell on private misgivings.

B. REVIEW A CLIENT'S VERSION OF EVENTS

Typically, a preparation meeting's main event consists of reviewing, updating and probing a client's version of events. Much time probably will have passed since you and a client discussed the case in detail. Thus, absent refreshment, a client's memory may be stale or incomplete. Moreover, in the interim, both you and a client are likely to have gained additional information. Some of this additional information may raise questions that you did not anticipate when you and a client last discussed the case in depth and may even appear to create gaps and/or inconsistencies in a client's account. Therefore, conducting a thorough review of a client's version of events can provide several benefits. For example:

- You may realize that you need to gather more information and/or documents before a deposition begins.
- Refreshing both your and a client's memory helps a practice question-answer session

proceed without repeated interruptions to clarify facts.

- At the deposition, you may recognize that a client's testimony is erroneous, and as a result you may give the client a chance to clarify and correct the erroneous testimony during the deposition.
- You may recognize that a client has failed to disclose helpful information that you want to add to the deposition record.

C. BRIEFLY EXPLAIN WHAT WILL OCCUR DURING THE DEPOSITION

Unless a client has previous deposition experience, you can also help to ease a client's anxiety by briefly explaining what will likely happen at the deposition. Your explanation may cover such matters as:

- Who will be present.
- That the client will be placed under oath, just as in court.
- That the deposing lawyer will probably begin by explaining the deposition procedures and asking questions about any medications or drugs the client may be taking.
- That after the deposing lawyer asks questions, you will have a chance to ask questions to clarify any evidence that may have come out muddled and to bring out helpful information that the deposing lawyer neglected to ask about.

When potentially sensitive or embarrassing subjects are relevant to a case, and therefore are likely to be inquired into by deposing counsel, you might also advise a client to expect such inquiries. For example, in a sexual harassment case in which your client contends that she was touched inappropriately at work, you might advise the client to expect detailed questioning about such matters as exactly where she was touched and how she reacted to being touched.

For clients that haven't had any deposition experience, it may also be helpful to show them a short video of an excerpt from a deposition.

D. EXPLAIN THE "GOLDEN RULES" FOR ANSWERING QUESTIONS

Clients often are unsure of how they are supposed to answer questions at deposition. To help clients understand the basic lay of the deposition land and perhaps correct any misperceptions they may have, explain the following "golden rules" before beginning to ask practice questions.

- **"Answer Honestly"**

This rule may seem self-evident and thus unnecessary to articulate. However, the advice can usefully remind clients that they should not try to outsmart the adversary's lawyer by either withholding or inventing information. Let the client know that they should tell the truth, whether that truth is good or bad.

- **"If You Don't Know or Don't Remember, Say So"**

This bit of advice is consistent with the earlier reminder to "answer honestly." Here, you remind clients that answers such as "I don't know" and "I don't remember" may be truthful. Such advice may be particularly valuable when questions ask for information that clients don't know but think they ought to know. For example, a client who actively participated in a meeting may think that she should remember what was discussed. Rather than look foolish by truthfully confessing to a lack of memory, the client may guess at what probably happened. Letting the client know it is okay to say "I don't know" can avoid creating problems down the line.

- **"If You Don't Understand the Question, Say So"**

Daily life socializes us to guess at the meaning of ambiguous questions. As a result, clients may guess at the meaning of deposition questions rather than tell deposing counsel that they don't understand the question. For example, a client who isn't sure which meeting an attorney is asking about may assume that the question pertains to a "June 8 meeting." If the client's guess is incorrect, the client may give erroneous testimony. Letting the client know that it is okay to say "I don't understand what you are asking" can help avoid such problems.

- **"Don't Provide Incomplete Answers That Are Literally True but Misleading"**

Despite your admonition to answer questions honestly, some clients may be tempted to withhold information by providing only partial, and misleading, answers. Consider the following example:

> Deposing Lawyer: Let's turn to the meeting that occurred on May 4th. Tell me what Mr. Jones said at that meeting about delivery dates.
>
> Client: He said that the computers would be delivered by September 17th.

Assume that the client remembers that what Jones said at the May 4th meeting was, "We'll have the computers delivered by September 17th if we can get the hard drives from the supplier in Korea by the first of September. But if we can't, we may not be able to make delivery until the beginning of November." The client may privately congratulate himself on hiding information while giving a technically accurate answer. However, partial, misleading answers such as these may damage a client's credibility with a judge or jury. For example, the client may be impeached with the deposition testimony at trial if he includes Jones' entire statement in his trial testimony. Similarly, other witnesses or documents may contradict the client's deposition testimony. Finally, deposing counsel may conclude that "cute" answers such as the one above are likely to make the client a poor trial witness and in any settlement negotiations discount much of what the client says.

Consequently, this golden rule encourages clients to provide complete answers to deposition questions.

- **"Do Not Volunteer"**

In general, you do not want clients volunteering information beyond that called for by a question. The volunteered information may be harmful to your case. However, even if the information is helpful, it may be information that you would prefer that a client not disclose in the absence of a question that requires its disclosure. The dialogue below demonstrates how you might provide advice when a client volunteers information during a practice session.

1. Q: They told you that the hard drives might not be delivered by the 17th of September, didn't they?

2. A: They did say that, but since at that time we had plenty of inventory on hand, we weren't that focused on the precise delivery date.

3. You (Comment): Mario, remember the golden rule "do not volunteer"? I think your answer goes beyond what you were asked. A "yes" answer would have been a complete answer to the question. You didn't need to volunteer the other information about the inventory and the precise delivery dates. When you are at the deposition, try to listen to questions and give complete answers but don't volunteer by going beyond the scope of what you're asked. You don't have to worry about getting out all the important information when

their lawyer is questioning you. Remember, if we need to bring out any additional information, we'll have an opportunity to do so later.

E. DISCUSS OBJECTIONS AND INSTRUCTIONS NOT TO ANSWER

Explain that you may object to questions, and that if you do so, you will probably advise the client to answer them anyway. Based on examples of trials in popular culture, deponents who lack deposition experience tend to expect that objected-to questions need not be answered. Thus, your explanation is likely to avoid client confusion at deposition.

You might also explain that on some occasions it might be necessary for you to instruct a client not to answer a question. Simply indicate that if you do so, the client should refuse to answer the question based on your advice.

Finally, you should explain to your client that they should pause briefly before answering questions to give you time to make an objection or an instruction not to answer.

F. CONDUCT A PRACTICE SESSION

Practice sessions are an essential aspect of preparing clients for depositions. During practice sessions, you ask clients to respond to questions that you believe deposing counsel is likely to ask. Thus, practice sessions give clients a realistic and concrete preview of what will happen at deposition. At the same time, such sessions give you a chance to educate clients about how to translate their knowledge of a case into effective answers. The subsections below explore strategies for conducting useful practice sessions.

1. Devote Practice Questioning to Selected Topics

Time considerations are likely to necessitate limiting practice questioning to selected topics. The topics should be those that you believe deposing counsel is almost certain to cover as well as those that you consider significant. When possible, include in a practice session a variety of questions that include both topics that are likely to produce testimony harmful to your case as well as topics that are likely to produce helpful testimony.

2. Ask Questions as Deposing Counsel

A practice session largely consists of your asking questions that you anticipate opposing counsel will ask at deposition and having clients answer as they would at deposition. For example, you may use leading questions and press for details that opposing counsel is likely to pursue.[4]

---

[4] You might even adopt an aggressive or even hostile tone during practice questioning. Doing so has risks and benefits. A client may benefit from such realistic practice. On the other hand, some clients may become terrified of the upcoming deposition or get the sense that you no longer have faith in their case. If you do want a client to experience a hostile questioning manner and if resources permit, consider preserving rapport by having a colleague who does not know the client play the role of deposing counsel.

Before embarking on practice questioning, advise clients that you will temporarily be assuming the role of deposing counsel when asking practice questions. For example, you may say something along these lines:

> Now that you have some idea of what will take place in the deposition, I want to give you an opportunity to practice answering questions. I'll play the role of opposing counsel and I'll ask you questions in the way they are likely to question you. Please answer as though this were the actual deposition. As you respond, I may step out of this role play and make a few suggestions. We won't have time to cover everything that opposing counsel is going to ask about, but this practice session will give you a pretty good sense of what to expect.

3. Improve Answers with Feedback and Advice

As a practice session unfolds, you should step out of the role of deposing counsel to provide feedback and advice that may improve clients' deposition performance. The subsections below describe advice and feedback that you may want to give.

- **Reinforce Golden Rules**

Often, you can improve upon a client's answer simply by reinforcing a golden rule. Illustrating a golden rule in a concrete context tends to help clients understand how to apply the rule. For example:

1. Q: Let's turn to the meeting that occurred on May 4th. Tell me what Mr. Jones said at that meeting about delivery dates.

2. A: He said that the computers would be delivered by September 17th.

3. Q: Now, that answer is technically accurate, but as I understand from what you told me earlier, it may not be complete. My understanding is that at the May 4th meeting, Jones said something like the computers would be delivered by September 17th if they could get the hard drives from the supplier in Korea by the first of September. And Jones said that if they couldn't get the hard drives, delivery might not be made until the beginning of November. Is my understanding correct?

4. A: Yes, but I wasn't sure that I was supposed to say all that.

5. Q: That's okay, that's why we're doing this practice session. Remember the golden rule "Answer Questions Completely"? If you have more information that responds to a question, go ahead and mention it. You want to try to give a complete answer to each question. So let's try that question again. . .

- **Suggest Appropriate Responses**

You can sometimes improve upon clients' answers by advising them of what information to include in their answers. Assuming that your advice is based on information that a client has previously disclosed, this strategy is ethically proper.

Example

1. Q: How did the lack of heat in the apartment affect your children?

2. A: They were really suffering during most of March.

3. You (Comment): John, if you're asked about how the lack of heat affected the kids, you really want to talk about the problems that you told me about earlier. In whatever words you want to use, you should talk about the kids missing school due to colds and infections, and the effect of the dampness on Marcia's asthma.

As in this example, when suggesting appropriate responses, you might also mention that clients need not parrot your exact words. Otherwise, you may overburden clients and inhibit them from testifying naturally and effectively.

- **Provide Both Positive and Negative Feedback**

Try to make sure you do not provide only negative feedback. You want the client to leave your preparation session and go into the actual deposition feeling confident, so look for things you can positively reinforce throughout the session as well as things you can help them improve upon.

Additionally, realize, that under the pressure of testifying at deposition, some clients are likely to have difficulty remembering and trying to apply your advice. If you overload clients with too many suggestions about how to answer questions, clients may focus too much on trying to remember your advice and too little on questions and their answers. Thus, try to focus on providing feedback on "big picture" issues that are more likely to be retained.

G. CONCLUDING PREPARATION SESSIONS

Before closing a preparation session, ask if the client has any questions or concerns. And then take a few moments to provide some common-sense final instructions. Typical concluding advice includes:

- Clients should not bring any documents to the deposition other than those you have indicated.
- If necessary, talk to clients about what to wear so that they will make a positive impression and feel appropriately dressed.
- Remind clients of exactly where and when a deposition will take place.
- Advise clients not to converse beyond normal social niceties "off the record" with opposing parties, deposing counsel, or anyone but you.
- Remind clients not to talk with friends or colleagues about: (1) the upcoming deposition, (2) the facts of the case, or (3) what took place during the preparation session. Discussions with friends and colleagues are usually not

privileged and may be inquired into during the deposition.

4. PREPARATION MEETINGS WITH NON-CLIENTS

This section examines strategies for preparing non-clients who are supportive of your client's position and are willing to meet with you. Such a non-client may be, for example, a lower echelon employee of a corporate client, or a bystander who observed an auto accident.

At the outset, realize that non-clients may be uncertain as to the legitimacy of meeting with you prior to deposition. They may also be uncertain about what to say if deposing counsel asks about what took place during the meeting. To reassure non-clients, you may begin a meeting by saying something along these lines:

> Mr. Williams, I appreciate your willingness to meet with me today. As you know, I'm the attorney for Susan French. First off, you should know that there's absolutely nothing wrong with us meeting in advance of your deposition. It's common and I simply want to answer any questions you may have about what will happen, and help you provide accurate testimony. There's nothing confidential about anything that I or you say, and if Ms. Asimow, the attorney who will be asking you questions, asks about whether we met and what was said between us, you can tell her exactly what we

talked about. Do you have any questions about this?[5]

Risks attend holding preparation meetings with non-clients. Since the meeting is not protected by the attorney-client privilege, anything that happens may be inquired into by the deposing attorney. Moreover, a deposing attorney may try to exploit the fact that you met to try to suggest that the non-client is biased.

Nonetheless, pre-deposition preparation meetings are often of benefit. Just as with clients, you may:

- Briefly explain what will take place at deposition, including that the fact that objected-to questions are normally to be answered. Such information is likely to ease the anxieties of non-clients who lack deposition experience.
- Review a non-client's version of events. So doing may refresh a non-client's recollection of helpful information. You may choose to elicit the information should deposing counsel's questions fail to do so.
- Explain the golden rules for answering questions. The information tends to help non-clients testify efficiently and accurately.

How much more you do at a preparation session is a matter of personal judgment. For example, do you want to conduct a practice session? Doing so may enable a non-client to testify more fully and

---

[5] Even experienced witnesses may need to be reminded of this absence of confidentiality.

accurately. On the other hand, practice sessions with non-clients are fraught with risk. Among the risks are the following:

- A non-client asked about what took place during a practice session may misinterpret your feedback and respond to deposition questions in a way that suggests that you tried to influence the non-client's deposition testimony during the practice session.
- You may inadvertently disclose strategies which a non-client later reveals to deposing counsel. For example, if deposing counsel asks a non-client to disclose the topics you reviewed during a practice session, the non-client's answers may reveal your litigation strategies.
- A non-client may interpret what you say in a practice session as an effort to influence their testimony, perhaps leading a non-client to backpedal on favorable testimony.

For all these reasons, you may not want to conduct practice sessions with non-clients. And should you choose to conduct a practice session, you may decide not to offer suggestions as to how a non-client should answer questions.

CHAPTER 17

DEPOSING FRIENDLY OR NEUTRAL WITNESSES

This Nutshell focuses primarily on depositions of adverse witnesses. But you may choose to depose a friendly or neutral witness when:

- The witness may be unavailable to testify by the time of trial. The deposition testimony may then be admissible in evidence at trial.
- The witness may align with an adversary and become a turncoat witness at trial. You may then use the deposition testimony to impeach the witness' changed testimony.
- You want to improve your settlement position by placing favorable evidence on the record.

1. PREPARATION STRATEGIES

Prepare for a deposition to preserve testimony and elicit a deponent's story as though you are preparing to conduct a deponent's direct examination at trial. For example, review the deponent's story in advance of the deposition. Refresh the witness' recollection with trial-related materials, but be aware that you may have to provide the materials to an adversary. Make sure the deponent is familiar with any exhibits to which you will refer during the deposition. Conduct a mock deposition before the real one takes place, providing feedback on the deponent's responses and including asking the deponent to respond to the adversary's likely cross examination questions.

2. BACKGROUND QUESTIONING

Just as though the deponent were testifying at trial, begin a deposition to preserve testimony by eliciting background evidence. At a deposition no less than at a trial, background questions tend to put deponents at ease. When a deposition substitutes for live testimony, information about a deponent's background reminds a judge or jury that the testimony emanates from a "real person." And background testimony can be particularly important when aspects of the background relate to a deponent's story. For example, a deponent's career as a minister may enhance the credibility of what took place during a religious service.

3. CONFORM TESTIMONY TO EVIDENCE RULES

At deposition, you have to be even more careful than at trial to conform your questions and a deponent's answers to evidence rules. You have to be your own "evidence judge," as an adversary who doesn't object at deposition may be able to do so when you seek to read deposition testimony into evidence at trial.[1] At deposition:

---

1 A common evidence rule allows lawyers to make "substantive" objections (e.g., objections based on the hearsay rule or character evidence rules) even if no objection was made at the earlier time when testimony was given.

- Include testimony that demonstrates a lay deponent's personal knowledge.
- Elicit foundational evidence, such as testimony showing that an exhibit is genuine, that a hearsay assertion is admissible, or that satisfies the basic facts of a presumption on which you rely.

4. RHETORICAL STORIES

Elicit a deponent's story in a way that is easy to follow and that emphasizes the rhetorical significance of important evidence. General strategies for doing so includes:

- Elicit events in chronological order.
- Ignore chronology in order to marshal together events that took place at disparate terms but that combine to enhance the probative value of important evidence.
- Enhance the credibility of a story, such as by asking a deponent to identify reasons for the deponent's ability to recall crucial events.
- Use both open and closed questions. Open questions ask deponents to describe important events in their own words, while closed questions allow you to elicit details about portions of a story that most strongly support your legal claims. You can also use

closed questions or documents to stimulate a forgetful deponent's recollection.[2]

- Enhance understanding of listeners with verbal "loops" that incorporate previously-given testimony into later questions. Example: "After you saw the bear go over the mountain, what's the next thing that happened?"
- Use the "No-No" strategy to emphasize what happened. Example:

  Q: Were all the king's horses at the scene?

  A: No.

  Q: Were all the king's men at the scene?

  A: No.

  Q: So who did come to Humpty's aid?

  A: Just a few horseback riders.

- Conclude testimony by asking a deponent to confirm particularly important information: "So to conclude, are you certain that the chicken came before the egg?"

The trial advocacy literature has many suggestions for effective witness examination strategies, and you may have developed your own. The important point is that many of the strategies that enhance the persuasiveness of in-court

[2] FRE 612 authorizes the use of documents (or other materials) to stimulate recall. An adversary's lawyer is however entitled to examine and introduce into evidence whatever you use to stimulate recollection.

examinations are also appropriate during depositions to preserve testimony.

5. OMITTING PORTIONS OF STORIES

Just as at trial, a deposition to preserve testimony is likely to involve decisions about what portions of a deponent's story you want to elicit. For instance, you might prefer not to elicit evidence of marginal relevance to your legal claims, or harmful evidence that your adversary may be unaware of.

A pre-deposition preparation session with a deponent is an opportunity to discuss issues such as these. And during the deposition, closed questions can help you navigate around portions of stories you want to avoid. For example, assume that a deponent participated in meetings 1, 2 and 3, and you want to elicit testimony only about meetings 1 and 3. After concluding questioning about meeting 1, you may ask the deponent, "Turning your attention now to meeting 3, can you tell us who beside yourself attended that meeting?"

6. REDIRECT EXAMINATION

After your examination concludes, your adversary has an opportunity to cross-examine the deponent. Following an adversary's examination, you may want to conduct redirect examination. As at trial, redirect at deposition allows you to respond to issues raised during your adversary's examination of the witness. For example, if opposing counsel obfuscates the order of events, on redirect you may review the proper chronology. Or if opposing counsel impeaches a deponent with a prior inconsistent statement, redirect examination is an opportunity for you to ask the deponent for an explanation.

INDEX

References are to Pages

ABOTA, 6

ADMISSIONS, REQUESTS FOR, 21

ADMONITIONS
Experts, depositions of, 229
Generally, 41–53, 74

AGGRANDIZE THE LIE, 142

ARGUMENTS, COMMUNICATING TO ADVERSARY, 125

AUTHENTICATING EXHIBITS, 166

BACKGROUND QUESTIONING
Experts, 231
Generally, 56–59
Internet search, 29
Neutral and friendly deponents, 290
Outline, 29

BEGINNING DEPOSITIONS, See generally, Chapter 4

BEHAVIOR OVER TIME, 143
Bicycling to work, do it!

BIAS
Experts, 233, 259–260
Generally, 57, 88, 131–132, 190, 286

BICYCLE COMMUTING, Good for health and planet

CEMENTING, See generally, Chapter 8

CHRONOLOGY
Clarifying, 123
Experts, 233

Practice and policies depositions, 216
Preparation, 22, 270
Timeline questioning, Chapter 5

CIVILITY, 3–8

CONCLUDING
Depositions, 59
Preparation sessions, 284

CONCLUSIONS
Evasive answers, 149
Experts, 234
Undermining, 143

COURT REPORTERS, 14–15, 39, 42, 45, 54, 60–61, 163–164, 167, 185, 193

CREDIBILITY
Background, 57
Experts, 231–232, 235
Historical reconstruction, 108
Internet search, 29
Neutral and friendly witnesses, 290, 291
Preparation, 27, 277
See generally, Chapter 9
T-Funnel, 77
"Why" questions, 112

CROSS EXAMINATION, 26–27, 127, 197, 290

DEFENDING DEPOSITIONS
Objections, See generally, Chapter 12
Protective orders, 6–7, 10, 14, 40, 96, 183, 189–190, 195–197, 209
Recess, 10, 195–196

DEMEANOR, 197

DIAGRAMS, 28, 161, 167–170

DOCUMENTS, See Chapter 11
Chronologies, 23, 30
Credibility challenge, 134–136
Experts, 234

Foundations, establishing, Chapter 11
Harmful, 36
Notice of deposition, 14
Outline, 34
Practice and policy depositions, 214, 223–225
Preparation, 21–22
Refreshing recollection, 53–55, 114, 155–159,161, 270, 289
Reviewing before deposition, 53–56, 269–272, 284
Stipulations, 40
Subpoena duces tecum, 13–15

"ESPECIALLY WHEN" TECHNIQUE, 109–110, 114

EVASIVE ANSWERS, See Chapter 10

"EXCEPT WHEN" TECHNIQUE, 109–110, 114, 141

FACTUAL CONTENTIONS
Experts, 25
Identifying, 17–20, 25, 32, 35

FORGETFUL DEPONENTS, See Chapter 10, See also MEMORY
Techniques for probing, 155–159

GENERALIZATIONS, See "ESPECIALLY WHEN" AND "EXCEPT WHEN"

GESTURES, CLARIFYING, 116–117

GOALS AT DEPOSITION
Deponent's version of events, obtaining, 2–3
Harmful evidence, uncovering & undermining, 2
Helpful evidence, obtaining and confirming, 2
Primary goals, 1–2

GOLDEN RULES, 275–279

GUESSING
Admonitions regarding, 43–44, 48–49

HARMFUL EVIDENCE
Undermining, See Chapter 9
Aggrandize the lie, 142–143

Attacking the inference, 140–142
Challenging accuracy of, 131–140
Checklist for undermining, 145–146
Opinions and conclusions, undermining, 143–145
Why search for, 2

HEARSAY
Asking for, 111, 225
Objecting to, 179, 180

HELPFUL ANSWERS
Cementing, See Chapter 8
Searching for, 2

HISTORICAL RECONSTRUCTION, 108–109

HYPER-TECHNICAL DEPONENTS, 152–154

"I DON'T KNOW" ANSWERS, See EVASIVE ANSWERS

"I DON'T REMEMBER" ANSWERS, See EVASIVE ANSWERS

IMPEACHMENT AT TRIAL, 60, 112, 119–20

IMPLAUSIBILITY, 138–139

IMPROPER BEHAVIOR BY OPPOSING COUNSEL, 193–196

INCONSISTENT STATEMENTS
Deponent's prior inconsistent statement, 136–137
Expert's prior inconsistent statements, 260
Third person's prior inconstant statement, 294

INSTRUCTIONS NOT TO ANSWER
Order to Compel an Answer, 191–193
Responding to invalid instructions, 184–191
Valid Grounds for, 183–184

LEADING QUESTIONS
Objections to, 174
To authenticate documents, 166
Use with forgetful deponent, 157
Use with T-Funnel questioning technique, 78

Use with timeline questioning technique, 64

LENGTH OF DEPOSITIONS, 9
Time limits on, 257–259, 382

MEMORY
Refreshing recollection during preparation session, 273
Techniques for refreshing deponent's recollection, 54, 78, 155

METHOD OF RECORDING TESTIMONY, 390

NEUTRAL WITNESS
Deposing, See Chapter 17
Preparing for deposition, 289

NON-RESPONSIVE ANSWERS, See ANSWERS

NOTE TAKING, 86

NOTICING DEPOSITIONS, See Chapter 2
Arranging for court reporter, 15
Contents of, 11
Location of depositions, 9
Number of depositions, 9
Method of recording testimony, 16
Production of documents at deposition, 14
When depositions can be taken, 12
Where depositions can be taken, 11
Who can be deposed, 9
Written notice required, 10

NUMBER OF DEPOSITIONS, 9

OBJECTIONS, See Chapter 12
Common objections, 172
    Curable objections, 172
        Argumentative, 176
        Assumes facts not in evidence, 174
        Compound, 174
        Inadmissible opinion, 177
        Lack of foundation, 176
        Lack of personal knowledge, 176
        Leading, 174

Mis-characterizes testimony, 175
Narrative, 175
Speculation, 176
Vague, 173
Non-curable objections, 178
Hearsay, 179
Inadmissible legal conclusion, 178
Irrelevant, 178
Privilege, 178
Disruptive objections, 180
Instructions not to answer, 183
Responding to improper instructions, 184
Objections used to coach deponent, 180
Obtaining answers to objectionable questions, 181
Responding to curable objections, 181
Speaking objections, 180

OPINIONS, 143

OPPOSING COUNSEL, 193

OUTLINES, 29–38

PARKING, 74, 86

PATH OF THE RIGHTEOUS, See "Pulp Fiction"

PERSON MOST KNOWLEDGEABLE, See Chapter 13

PRACTICE & POLICY DEPOSITIONS, See Chapter 14
Purposes of, 213
Questioning strategies during, 216, 223
Who to depose, 214

PREPARING TO TAKE A DEPOSITION, See Chapter 3
Chronology, 22
Crucial factual contentions, 17
Document review, 20
Factual contentions, 17
Outline, creating, 29
Steps in preparation, 17
Step 1, Identify crucial factual contentions, 17
Step 2, Identifying topics, events and materials, 20

Step 3, Prepare a deposition outline, 29

PREPARING WITNESSES FOR DEPOSITION, See Chapter 16
Non-clients, 285
Pre-meeting preparation, 269
Prepare case chronology, 270
Review document requests, 269
Tell client what documents to review, 271
Preparatory meeting topics, 272
Golden rules, 275
Objections, 279
Review client's version, 273
Suggesting appropriate responses, 282

PRESERVE TESTIMONY, See Chapter 17

PRIOR INCONSISTENT STATEMENTS, 136

QUESTIONING OWN CLIENT AT DEPOSITION, See Chapter 17

QUESTIONING TIPS, See Chapter 7

REFRESHING RECOLLECTION, 155

SETTLEMENT
Communicating arguments to enhance, 37, 125
Enhancing through professional demeanor, See Chapter 1

SEVEN HOUR RULE, 38, 39

STIPULATIONS, 39, 61

SUBJECT MATTER DEPOSITIONS, See Chapter 13
Limit on number, 200
Notice for, 200
Obtaining adverse party's contentions, limits on, 209
Scope of, 207
Why take, 199

SUPPLEMENTING DEPOSITION TESTIMONY, 60

SUSPENDING DEPOSITIONS
To seek order compelling an answer, 191

T-FUNNELS, See Chapter 6
Combining with timelines, 93
Common T-Funnels, 88
Event essential details, 89
Illustration of, 79
Inverted, 86
Parking, 86
Secondary, 84
Series of, 82

TIME LIMITS, 39

TIMELINES, See Chapter 5
Basic-timeline pattern, 64–69
Combining with T-Funnels, 93
Common problems and solutions to, 72–75
Gaps in, 67
Illustration of, 70
Obtaining details when chronology not available, 72, 100
Parking, 74

TIPS FOR EFFECTIVE QUESTIONING, See Chapter 7

UNDERMINING HARMFUL ANSWERS, See Chapter 9

UNCERTAIN DEPONENTS, See Chapter 10

WHO CAN BE DEPOSED, See NOTICING DEPOSITIONS
"Why" Questions, 111